WALL DISEASE

ALSO BY JESSICA WAPNER

The Philadelphia Chromosome:
A Genetic Mystery, a Lethal Cancer,
and the Improbable Invention
of a Lifesaving Treatment

WALL DISEASE

The Psychological Toll of Living Up Against a Border

JESSICA WAPNER

THE EXPERIMENT

NEW YORK

The Experiment, LLC
220 East 23rd Street, Suite 600
New York, NY 10010-4658
theexperimentpublishing.com

THE EXPERIMENT and its colophon are registered trademarks of The Experiment, LLC. Many of the designations used by manufacturers and sellers to distinguish their products are claimed as trademarks. Where those wdesignations appear in this book and The Experiment was aware of a trademark claim, the designations have been capitalized.

The Experiment's books are available at special discounts when purchased in bulk for premiums and sales promotions as well as for fund-raising or educational use. For details, contact us at info@theexperimentpublishing.com.

Library of Congress Cataloging-in-Publication Data

Names: Wapner, Jessica, author.
Title: Wall disease : the psychological toll of living up against a border / Jessica Wapner.
Description: New York : The Experiment, [2020] | Includes index.
Identifiers: LCCN 2020033011 (print) | LCCN 2020033012 (ebook) | ISBN 9781615197347 | ISBN 9781615197354 (ebook)
Subjects: LCSH: Walls--Psychological aspects. | Boundaries--Psychological aspects.
Classification: LCC JC323 .W37 2020 (print) | LCC JC323 (ebook) | DDC 320.1/2--dc23
LC record available at https://lccn.loc.gov/2020033011
LC ebook record available at https://lccn.loc.gov/2020033012

ISBN 978-1-61519-734-7
Ebook ISBN 978-1-61519-735-4

Cover design and illustration by Beth Bugler
Text design by Jack Dunnington
Author photograph by Daphne Vasilakis

Manufactured in the United States of America

First printing September 2020
10 9 8 7 6 5 4 3 2 1

To Lukas, Luke, and Daphne,
who light up the way

Contents

Introduction
Concrete, Steel, and Razor Wire

Governments typically justify border walls as a necessary measure for preventing illegal immigration, terrorism, or drug smuggling—or a combination of the three. There is little to no evidence that any border wall in the world accomplishes these feats. There is mounting evidence, however, that they cause harm. Many of the issues surrounding borders and their barriers are well known: family separation, deportation, denial of refuge. Less recognized, though, is the psychological peril of living up against a wall.

East Germans living close to the Berlin Wall were the first to name the problem: *Mauerkrankheit*, or wall disease.[1] In the early 1970s, German psychologist Dietfried Müller-Hegemann said the condition warranted its own diagnosis as a mental illness.[2] He described the case of a patient who developed a locked jaw and became suicidal after several stymied attempts to take a train into West Germany, where her husband was, as an example of the unique pathology of wall disease. The symptoms of wall disease included a sense of being locked up and of being isolated from friends and family. More severe cases stemming from the Berlin Wall could include psychosis, schizophrenia, and behavioral problems such as "alcoholism, anger, despondency, dejection and suicide," writes Cornell University sociologist Christine Leuenberger.

Müller-Hegemann saw the wall itself as the culprit behind the psychological disorders turning up in his clinic during those years. The repressive policies of the German Democratic Republic meant that he couldn't safely conduct studies that would have enabled him to prove his assertion, and his book on the diagnosis was published only after he emigrated. In the decades since, wall disease has remained an obscure phenomenon, known as a peculiar by-product of the Cold War rather than a widespread condition continuing to afflict people around the globe living near other border structures.

That view is inaccurate. An increasing body of research shows that the symptoms of wall disease are pervasive. The condition exists at the border between the US and Mexico, between India and Pakistan, on opposite sides of the peace lines of Northern Ireland. Where border walls exist, so does wall disease.

The symptoms of wall disease have become so entrenched in modern culture that we barely recognize them. People living near border walls often experience higher rates of depression than the regional population at large. They seem to believe the wall makes them safer, despite a lack of evidence. They experience "othering," that is, viewing those on the other side of the wall as alien and dangerous despite the lack of evidence supporting that view. Poverty rates are often high in borderland regions. The wall imposes its mass on the very brain cells of those living nearby, reshaping mental maps and, in turn, their view of the world around them.

The celebrations in Germany and around the globe following the fall of the Berlin Wall were about more than the ability to safely cross a border where a person once might have been shot for doing so. The West Germans clapping at cars arriving from East Germany on November 10, 1989, the day after the first gate was opened,[3] were applauding not just for those who'd been locked on the other side but also in the hope of a borderless world. Just weeks before the wall came down, its destruction had been "unthinkable," one local told newscaster Peter Jennings at the time. Its momentous ending sent out a worldwide wave of optimism about the shrinking need for borders and their government-sanctioned, armed patrollers.

Thirty years later, that elation is all but gone.[4] Border walls failed to disappear after Berlin's fell. Then came the September 11, 2001, terrorist attacks. In the decade that followed, forty-seven new border walls arose around the world. In the US, the Secure Fence Act of 2006 authorized the building of hundreds of miles of fencing along the border with Mexico, and it paved the way for a proliferation of new cameras, satellites, and drones for surveillance.[5] Today there are more than seventy significant security barriers at borders worldwide. "Walls have become a normalized response to insecurity," writes Élisabeth Vallet,[6] geographer and scientific director of geopolitics at the University of Quebec at Montreal. Each new wall makes the next one that much easier to justify and that much easier to generate support for.

The border wall between the US and Mexico has failed to accomplish the objectives that have been cited to justify its construction in recent years. It hasn't stopped undocumented immigrants from entering the US because most enter legally with visas that then expire. It hasn't stopped the flow of illegal drugs, the vast majority of which come through legal ports of entry. And US citizens, not international terrorists, have committed nearly all of the country's deadliest shootings in modern US history. The situation is similar worldwide. Although some border structures have achieved short-term peace in tumultuous situations, such outcomes are by far the exception and rarely long-lasting. What's far more evident is that border walls stir up animosity against those on the other side. Politicians know this, and some choose to exploit the us-them divisions for nationalist support.

Climate change will likely heighten tensions between people on opposite sides of border walls. Erosion of the riverbanks in Bangladesh already displaces up to two hundred thousand people per year. Scientists predict that sea levels there will rise by five to six feet within the next eighty years, a change that could push up to fifty million people out of their homes. The country's border with India, marked by a barbed wire–topped fence installed by India to keep Bangladeshi migrants out,[7] is one of the most violent in the world; as climate refugees seek safety,[8] it's easy to imagine it will only get worse.

COVID-19 is also solidifying borders worldwide—even those not marked by physical walls. In the spring of 2020, dozens of countries around the world were shut to incoming foreigners. As the pandemic proceeded,[9] the number of countries closing their borders increased across the globe. Countries within the European Union shut themselves to one another. The US closed its borders with Mexico and Canada. (And, in a reversal from history, Mexican officials have called for tighter restrictions on Americans entering their country. The COVID-19 pandemic made American passports a liability rather than an asset—and demonstrated how quickly border politics can flip-flop.) Nearly all entry into China was forbidden. Only commercial traffic could pass into Saudi Arabia. In June 2020, nearly two hundred countries remained completely or partially closed, and only twenty-two countries had no travel restrictions.[10] These rules may not be tied to concrete walls and concertina wire, but they reflect a growing mindset that sees borders as dangerous. It's easy to imagine that some of these security measures may become the new normal, outlasting COVID-19.

All of which is to say: Border walls are here to stay and will likely become even more prominent in years to come if the world remains on its current political, environmental, and health trajectories. "We're entering a severe crisis," geographer Gerard Toal told me, "of the very nature of human settlement on Earth."

Lost in the discourse surrounding border walls is what happens to the people living up against them. How are their lives and livelihoods affected by the concrete and steel barricades fixed into the ground near their homes and workplaces? What is it like to walk by a giant fence radiating messages that trigger fear and insecurity every day? How does living by a border wall change people? Occasionally, the plight of indigenous tribes whose ancestral lands straddle the US-Mexico border makes national headlines. Otherwise, borderlands people remain largely forgotten in the national and global conversation.

The price of our inattention is a silent scourge of subtle but nonetheless very real mental health issues. The evidence establishing clear links between border walls and the psychological toll they exact on people living in their shadows is now undeniable. From the way walls distort our perception of our surroundings to the fear we experience when we see coils of barbed wire; from the depression stemming from restricted movement to that caused by the structure's sheer ugliness—it's impossible not to have a psychological response to a border wall.

We don't know the full extent of this crisis; we likely never will. Genetics, support networks, and an exceedingly complicated web of other factors shape how we respond to mental adversity. No large-scale study could ever claim to know what, if any, mental health issues borderlands people endure on an individual level. But there are clear patterns of psychological harm among populations living near border walls around the world. These people face inordinate challenges researchers are only just beginning to grasp and that we can no longer ignore.

It was through my work as a science journalist that I first learned about Mauerkrankheit. The phenomenon made me wonder if other border walls elicited the same troubling thought patterns and behaviors. That question led to an article (published in 2019) about how border walls change the way we think. But more in-depth examination seemed warranted. Here, a worldwide trend in mental health was affecting an increasing number of people, and so few of us seemed aware of it. Scientists from a wide range of fields are studying these barriers and just beginning to understand the connections between the brain, our emotions, and the many other dynamics at play in our experience with border walls. It takes time for data to become conclusive. But the walls don't wait for that. They'll be erected regardless of the many hints of the psychological damage they are causing, if the officials we've elected so choose.

In the chapters that follow, I'll unpack the research behind these trends of harm—the neuroscience, the psychology, the biology, the sociology, and the geography. I come to this not as an expert in any of these fields but as a journalist determined to understand how the multitude of border walls now standing around the globe are reshaping the human psyche. These issues transcend politics because they aren't about any particular wall or any particular country. Every border structure has its own history, its own circumstances, and its own implications. But wall disease can afflict anyone living in a borderland anywhere in the world. This book isn't about politics; it's about humans.

We are all born into a world in which we involuntarily belong to a nation that exists somewhere in the global pecking order. Sometimes it's not even clear whether a particular population saw themselves as a cohesive group before someone drew a line on a map to separate one piece of the planet from another. The border between the US and Mexico arose from a hungry vision of continent-wide expansion, the belief that the land and its resources can be owned, and a disregard for the psychological fallout of the actions that followed that vision and belief. It is the case at so many borders around the world.

In a world so invested in border walls, we must confront the uncomfortable fact that these structures are causing insidious mental health issues in people who are often powerless to do anything about them. Ultimately the afflicted population extends far beyond the borderlands of the world. Most of us are unaware of the extent to which we carry the artificial construction of national borders in our minds and how they shape the way we think about the world and our place within it.

Which is to say, maybe we all have a bit of wall disease.

1

Sliding Down the Levee on Cardboard

A Visit to Brownsville, Texas

ON FEBRUARY 2, 1848, a negotiator appointed by President James Polk named Nicholas Trist met with several Mexican diplomats in Villa de Guadalupe Hidalgo, a neighborhood in the northern area of Mexico City. The area had first become famous among Mexicans three hundred years earlier when Juan Diego, an indigenous Mexican rumored to be an Aztec prince who had converted to Roman Catholicism,[1] had a vision of the Virgin Mary. He received a message with the vision telling him that a shrine should be built on a nearby hill. After the church was built, Juan Diego lived in a hut next door and took care of pilgrims. He was beatified in 1990, Pope John Paul II confirmed his sainthood in 2002, and the Basilica of Guadalupe is still considered the holiest church in Mexico.[2] Every place has a history.

But religion wasn't what had brought Trist and his counterparts to this place. They were there to sign a piece of paper that would officially end the war between their two countries.

To the victor went the spoils. The Treaty of Guadalupe Hidalgo granted the United States about half of the territory belonging to Mexico. The land amounted to more than

525,000 square miles—land that included most or all of present-day Arizona, California, western Colorado, Nevada, New Mexico, Texas, and Utah—enabling the US to just about fully realize its vision of expanding across the continent. Mexico also agreed to recognize the Rio Grande as its northern boundary, a contentious issue that had helped precipitate the Mexican War in the first place. In exchange the US agreed to pay Mexico $15 million and to pay off $3.25 million in claims that US citizens had against Mexico. Mexican citizens living in areas that abruptly belonged to the US upon the signing of the treaty could either relocate or become American citizens.[3] Despite these seemingly favorable terms, President Polk was angry with Trist because he had ignored the president's order to return home almost four months earlier and instead remained in Mexico. That made Trist a rogue diplomat negotiating illegally behind the president's back in order to end the war.[4] And Polk had wanted more territory, Baja California, which is still part of Mexico.

According to Trist's wife, Virginia Randolph Trist (a granddaughter of Thomas Jefferson), just as Trist was about to put pen to paper, Don Bernardo Couto, a Mexican signer, said to him, "This must be a proud moment for you; no less proud than it is humiliating for us." Trist replied, "We are making peace, let that be our only thought." But he had more to say years later to his wife. "Could those Mexicans have seen into my heart at that moment, they would have known that my feeling of shame as an American was far stronger than theirs could be as Mexicans," he wrote her in a letter in 1864.[5] "For though it would not have done for me to say so there, that was a thing for every right minded American to be ashamed of, and I was ashamed of it, most cordially and intensely ashamed of it." The maneuverings behind this extraordinary land grab had left him with severe misgivings. "Had my course at such moments been governed by my conscience as a man, and my sense of justice as an individual American," Trist wrote his wife, "I should have yielded in every instance."[6]

The treaty established the westernmost boundary between the two countries at three nautical miles south of the southern tip of San Diego Bay. The line then proceeds east toward Yuma, Arizona, southeast toward Nogales, Mexico, and east to El Paso, Texas. From there, the border follows a jagged southeastern path of the Rio Grande to Brownsville, Texas, where it ends at the six hundred thousand square miles of deep blue water that make up the Gulf of Mexico.

A pile of rocks—no fence, no wall—marked the western edge of the border after the treaty signing. In 1894, the rocks were replaced by a twenty-foot obelisk known as Monument 258: the last in a line of such monuments along the border—pushpins on an otherwise invisible line. Years later, a fence was built to mark this western spot, placed a few feet north of the monument, putting the obelisk squarely in Mexico, in the border town of Playas de Tijuana. Later, the public areas where people meet on both sides of the wall, which encompass the monument, were collectively named Friendship Park, or El Parque de la Amistad.[7]

The border was haphazardly patrolled until the Immigration Acts of 1921 and 1924, which sought to limit the number of people entering the country, a restriction that led to a rise in illegal crossings. In 1924, the federal government established the Border Patrol to combat that influx,[8] supplying a badge and a revolver to its 450 agents, along with hay and oats for their horses. The militarization of the border as we know it now largely began in the 1990s, under the Clinton administration. Operation Hold the Line, started in 1993 in El Paso, Texas, deterred border-crossers with a show of force. A year later, the government launched Operation Gatekeeper, a program focused on the half-million people illegally crossing from Tijuana, Mexico, into San Diego, California, every year.[9] Border Patrol became part of the US Department of Homeland Security in 2003, when politicians were still addressing (and capitalizing on) 9/11-spurred concerns about terrorism. The US government currently spends $4.7 billion on border patrol every year[10] and employs more than twenty-three thousand agents.

Reverend John Fanestil began offering Communion at the fence in Friendship Park in 2008. On the other side, Pastor Guillermo Navarrete did the same. At that time, the slats in the border fence were far enough apart that people could fit their hands between them. Reverend Fanestil would dip bread in a cup of red wine and pass pieces of it through the fence into Mexico, so that worshippers on both sides could eat from a single loaf.

The US side of Friendship Park was closed for construction soon after the Communions started. Eventually the San Diego Border Patrol agreed to open the area for four hours on Saturdays and Sundays. Reverend Fanestil has been there every Sunday since November 2011. He no longer hands wine-dipped bread to the other side because US Customs law now forbids passing anything through the wall. And even without that restriction, the tight metal grid that has replaced the slats is too small for anything larger than a fingertip. The fence is more like a fine mesh screen, making it impossible to see clearly to the other side.

On one typical weekend day, a woman on the US side sat in a camping chair with a baby on her lap, the stroller parked next to her. A man in jeans and a T-shirt leaned right up against the metal, his hands in his pockets, talking to a silhouette with a handbag on the other side. A few feet away, the scene repeated: a man up against the fence, a silhouette on the other side doing the same. Near the end of the area accessible to the public, two women sat on the ground facing Mexico. A boy in a black T-shirt and red shorts stood next to them. It may have been their parents on the other side, their bodies obscured by the matrix of metal. No one could take a good look at each other. They could touch their fingertips together, nothing more.

Yolanda Varona, who was separated from her children when she was deported in 2010,[11] attends Mass at the Border Church, La Iglesia Fronteriza, on the Tijuana side of Friendship Park, every Sunday. She prays for an end to the wall, which, she says in a 2016 video about the church, "has only caused separation, death, and a lot of sadness." At the end of every service, worshippers are invited to approach the wall. On the Mexican side, dozens of people walk to the metal grid. "We're trying to take this wall and turn it into a ta-

ble," Reverend Fanestil told me. He believes that when people come together in this way, they diminish the oppressive
power of this separator. The worshippers put their fingers to
the tiny holes and those on the other side do the same. The
leaders on both sides speak into their microphones: "Amen."

One of the stranger aspects of the border wall between
Brownsville, Texas, and Matamoros, Mexico—its sister city,
just across the bridge over the Rio Grande—is how innocent
it looks. I had expected to see a solid, forbidding structure
looming over its immediate area like a giant highway barrier
ready to crush whoever stood in its unforgiving presence. I
thought I would feel intimidated standing beside it, even just
looking at it from a distance. But when I finally stood there,
face to face with it on a warm spring night, I felt like I was
looking through a fence into a park. I had to confirm with
someone on the street that this was actually the border wall.
I had come to Brownsville in March 2020, just before non-
essential travel came to a virus-induced halt, to see the border for myself. I wanted to speak in person with people living
at the border wall. I wanted to hear how it affected them to
have in their own backyards the barrier that was at the center
of a country-dividing debate. I wanted to stand in front of a
building when the slanted shadows of the barrier's steel bollards fell across the bricks in the late afternoon sun. I wanted
to talk with scholars who'd grown up in the area and had
thought deeply about the identity of a person born and bred
in *la frontera*, the borderlands. I wanted to witness life up
against a wall, even if only briefly. What I encountered there

transformed my understanding of what it means to be part of a nation, and confirmed the pressing need to weigh the psychological toll of border walls when we consider their value.

I couldn't even make it out of the airport without encountering the first of many indelible stories from lives spent near the border. When I'd mentioned my research to the car rental agent, she suggested I visit a clothing store across the street from the wall. Then she shared a memory: As a student at the University of Texas Rio Grande Valley, which is at the edge of town, she'd been sitting in the recreation center one day when a bullet flew through the window. "The shooting was in Mexico and the bullet landed in the United States," she said.

Standing outside Ross, the store she'd recommended, I saw how easily that could happen. The wall of windows looked directly out at the wall of steel. But when I asked the security guard, a twenty-one-year-old named Israel Yañez, about what it was like to stare at a giant fence all day, he said he barely noticed it. He thought the same was likely true for everyone shopping at the store, all of whom were speaking Spanish. "Really?" I asked him. "You don't notice it?" Well, he told me, there was that time a bunch of people rushed across the international bridge from Matamoros, less than a quarter mile from the store, and the police sprayed them with tear gas. And there was the night when his mother, waiting for Yañez to finish his shift, saw a Border Patrol van go the wrong way down a one-way street, round up two dozen or so people who had been hiding in the dark, and force them inside the vehicle, which, he told me, locals refer to as "the dog pound." This, in the shadow of the wall that Yañez described as a routine part of life. It reminded me of the process of normalization that often accompanies repetitive trauma[12]: We act as if everything is fine, when it most definitely is not. Sufferers of abuse may do this, pretending that life at home is peaceful, even convincing themselves that a harmful dynamic is nothing out of the ordinary. Of course, staring at a border wall during work is a very distant cry from the severe, harmful, and dangerous circumstances that a family might ignore in order to appear normal to themselves and others. But the nonchalance with which Yañez spoke about the border wall seemed strikingly at odds with its purpose. Was that a sign of resilience, or had he become numb to the reality of his surroundings?

In Mission, Texas, about an hour from Brownsville, cousins Reynaldo, or Rey, Anzaldua and Jose Alfredo, or Fred, Cavazos were more outspoken about the trouble the border wall has brought to their lives. Cavazos, his sister, Eloisa, and many of their cousins own just less than seventy acres of land along the shore of the Rio Grande (Eloisa owns just over half, with the remainder spread equally among the others). The US government wants to build a wall on it, adding to the 650 miles of barriers already in place along the northern edge of Mexico.[13]

In the summer of 2018, the family began receiving letters from the government requesting "right of entry" for twelve months for a payment of one hundred dollars. The family refused access and a federal court eventually increased the payment to $450, Anzaldua tells me. Toward the end of 2019, the government offered the family about $400,000 for six acres of their property, says Anzaldua. Eloisa has refused the offer so far. The family expects that eventually the government will seize their property through eminent domain. Anzaldua says they've known since the beginning of this ordeal that the government will eventually take their land. "We know we're going to lose this," he says. But they are holding out hope that the next administration may not pursue the takeover—and also fighting back as a matter of principle.

I followed Anzaldua and Cavazos on a drive across the property. Behind small weekend cabins with swing sets and hammocks, the Rio Grande looked deceptively peaceful; the current is strong beneath the surface. We parked at the end of their property and talked while the wind blew across the dirt and dry grass that forms the shore. A pile of rubble containing chunks of concrete and errant wires spoke of recent demolition, though its origins were unclear. A border guard sat inside a government vehicle a few feet from us, parked under a wooden canopy. Behind us, a surveillance tower rose twenty feet in the air on top of a crane staked into the ground. And beyond the tower, a long row of silver steel poles stretched into the distance, parallel to the river, at the edge of a six-thousand-acre sugarcane farm. This eighteen-foot-high wall was built with private funds raised by a Florida nonprofit founded by an Iraq War veteran. The wall is so close to the water that it will likely disrupt the normal flow of seasonal floodwaters, sending the water straight onto the family's land instead of across the riverfront portion of the farm.

Against this militarized backdrop, they told their family story. Anzaldua, Cavazos, and Eloisa were raised on the land we stood on. Their grandmother, who purchased the land in the 1950s, would bring them there regularly, telling them she was going to teach them how to work. They used bamboo poles to fish and fed the cows she raised for meat. Cavazos, seventy-one, a wheelchair user, and Eloisa, sixty-nine, who is partially deaf, now depend on rental income from the weekend cabins, amounting to about thirty thousand dollars per year, and other minor income from the property, to support themselves. And their family has lived in the region since the Spanish settled the area in the 1750s, when the King of Spain granted six hundred thousand acres of land that is now in southern Texas to their Mexican ancestor, José Narciso Cavazos. (We'll set aside the possibility that, perhaps, the land wasn't the king's to give in the first place.) Cavazos and his sister inherited the property from their grandmother, who told them, "Never sell a piece of land. The land will feed you." The fight to save their small patch of Texas has taken over their lives. Anzaldua, seventy-five, has joined their effort not only because they're family but also because he despises what the government is trying to do. They speak with journalists any chance they can, and Cavazos testified before Congress alongside several other people whose land has been swept up in the border wall initiative. The land, they told me, is their last connection to their ancestry. "It's not about the money," said Anzaldua, "it's about our love of the land."

Anzaldua and Cavazos, whose Mexican ancestors became US citizens through the Treaty of Guadalupe Hidalgo that ended the Mexican–American War, say the invasion of the government into their land is racist. "People think we're for-eigners," Anzaldua, who is about one third American Indi-an, told me. Anzaldua, who fought in the Vietnam War and whose uncle, Fred and Eloisa's father, served in World War II under General Patton, believes his family is not receiving the equal protection guaranteed by the Fourteenth Amend-ment, because they are perceived as Mexican—or somehow less American than his fellow citizens. He questions whether the government would be pushing for right of entry if the owners were white. "Are we less Texan?" he said.

Even though they stood on the US side of the wall, Anz-aldua and Cavazos had become "the other," the ones who don't belong and aren't allowed. As we stood conversing on the tan earth that had been in their family for seventy years, hard-won by their pioneering grandmother, rich soil hidden beneath the dry surface, their words reminded me of what psychiatrist Vamik Volkan, who specializes in international conflicts, had told me about walls and group identity. "There are realistic issues at the Mexican border, but it is all psy-chological," he said. "The reason is not to protect yourself from physical invasion, it is to protect yourself from a psy-chological invasion against your identity." The government's efforts to build a wall on their land had alienated Anzaldua and Cavazos from their own country. The fact that their American roots extended back generations, that they were veterans, that their presence harmed no one made the efforts to co-opt their land for a border wall that much more egre-gious to them. They believe those who built the private wall neighboring their land and the US government see them as belonging on the opposite side of the border. It's a mindset that hovers among people living at borders around the world and that creates insecurity, anxiety, and depression, all components of wall disease.

Ten minutes away, the National Butterfly Center welcomes "winter Texans" (retirees from the northern part of the state) and tourists wanting to glimpse any of the 230 species of butterflies that have been spotted at the 100-acre, privately owned nature preserve since it opened in 2002. As we sat on a stone bench, a red-bordered pixie butterfly making itself at home on a guamuchil tree behind us, Luciano Guerra, sixty-three, who works as a photographer and educator at the center, told me about how, when he was growing up in this town, children would be sent to the principal's office for a paddling if they spoke Spanish in class. "It made you wonder what's wrong with speaking Spanish," he said. "That's our family, our tradition, our heritage."

Guerra and his father were both born in Texas, but the rest of his family—his mother and three older siblings—were born in Mexico and were not US citizens until later in life. Crossing the border was not a big deal when he was growing up. Guerra's family and many others considered the people across the river to be their neighbors, and they regularly walked over to Mexico for nights out.

In 2019, the National Butterfly Center won a battle to stop construction of a border wall through their land.[14] The state district court of Texas ruled that none of the money appropriated by Congress for a border wall could be used to build the structure through the middle of the center, or through the nearby Santa Ana National Wildlife Refuge or the historic La Lomita Chapel. But this decision doesn't guarantee protection. If the president declares a state of emergency over border issues, any funds he draws on would not be subject to these exemptions.

With the same insecurity plaguing Rey Anzaldua and Fred Cavazos, Guerra worries that it's only a matter of time. A border wall would devastate the center, he says. Just a small fraction of the original native habitat of the Rio Grande Valley, where the National Butterfly Center sits, currently remains, and most of it is along the river, the only source of fresh water in the region. When the wall is built, some animals will be stuck on the river side of it, unable to return to their homes. Others will be cut off from water. Nocturnal animals will be disrupted by the floodlights shining from the wall onto the river and the shore beyond. He also believes people won't be as interested in the center anymore because they won't feel safe walking the grounds, much of which will be accessible only through a gate in the wall. Guerra is a Republican who voted for Trump in 2016 and had never engaged in any activism until he was faced with the prospect of a border wall running through a place that has brought so much meaning to his life and so much joy to the children he speaks with on school field trips, many of whom arrive scared of nature.[15] "We can see a change in them by the time they leave," he told me. Guerra also said that even if the center remains protected from wall construction, he will still continue to fight against it. He has the same determination to push back against oppression that I saw in Anzaldua and Cavazos.

"We don't think anybody should get a border wall," he said. "We don't think it's necessary and we know the damage it's going to do elsewhere."

The time I spent talking with Guerra had underscored something I'd noticed since arriving in Brownsville. He had spoken about how blended his life was with Mexico growing up, and that was exactly how Brownsville felt: like a blend of two countries. Everyone spoke Spanish in the restaurants I went to; I felt like a foreigner who didn't speak the native language. In the bread aisle of a supermarket I'd stopped at, coolers filled with tortillas dropped off fresh each day lined several shelves. It was also a typical American city, with its highway lit by signs from chain restaurants in strip malls off the service roads. These sights and moments clarified what the border wall between Brownsville and Matamoros really is: an artificial construction intended to make people feel separate from one another. Brownsville may be a borderland, but the border isn't the sharp line of a map. It's a wide gradient where the worlds on either side coexist. The division between the two countries might be valid politically but the land and the people don't make that distinction. "Walls protect large group identity, and in turn personal identity feels more secure," Vamik Volkan had told me, "but of course, it is a psychological illusion." And that illusion distorts perceptions within the US, leaving citizens of Mexican heritage feeling like outsiders when in truth, even those across the border don't qualify for that label. In Brownsville, it was clear that the separation between the US and Mexico exists only in people's minds. Brownsville is not alone. Paranoia about the dangerous "other" and false divisions are two forms that wall disease takes in borderlands throughout the world.

On the other side of the wall separating Texas from Mexico, though, division no longer feels like an illusion. It feels bitingly real. Walking into Mexico is easy. Four quarters gets you through the turnstile at the start of the bridge from Brownsville to Matamoros. The line to enter the country, if there is one, moves quickly. The X-ray machine for scanning bags isn't always on and, instead, guards conduct cursory bag inspections similar to what you'd encounter at a museum.

The pleasantly smooth entry into Mexico made stepping into Matamoros that much more shocking. There I was, an American in a foreign country, as if I'd been invited to visit. And on the hillside, fewer than one hundred yards away from the guard who stirred his flashlight around my bag and waved me through, thousands of asylum seekers from Mexico and points south were waiting for their asylum requests to be granted. Their tents, most of which were covered in garbage bags for extra protection against the elements, were packed right up against each other, like a Lego construction made of only the smallest cubes. Everyone was using porta-potties for toilets. Stations of them were lined up along the camp. At one, a woman handed out toilet paper to those in need. Groups of children walked back and forth along the main dirt path, some in shoes and some not. As I walked through the camp, I passed an adult kicking a soccer ball with a small child. Thin pieces of meat charring on makeshift grills gave the camp the tempting smell of a big barbecue, belying the deprivation evident in the surroundings. In an open area, several people waited under a white tent for medical attention at mobile health units parked in the camp for the foreseeable future. Farther down the path, a group of people convened on a ledge to learn English from a woman with tattoos. "It is a strawberry," they all said at once. Near them, another cluster of people hovered around a charging station.

A twenty-year-old from Honduras who had left his home to escape violence and poverty told me that he'd been living in the camp for a year. Every day he hoped for news about his asylum application, and every night he went to sleep frustrated. He wouldn't leave, though, he said. Several young girls played with jump ropes near the UNICEF tent. One girl's long, tidy braid made me wonder about who had taken the care to do that and whether it was the work of a mother trying to keep life as normal as possible. The girls skipped rope for a while and then sat on the ground, turning the ropes into pretend snakes.

Back at the bridge, the line to get into the United States was long and slow, for both pedestrians and drivers. I started worrying about my parking meter expiring before I got back to the other side where I'd left my car, but then a woman who was clearly American breezed past me and I realized that I was standing in the line for Mexican citizens. I switched lines, and less than a minute later, a passport control officer was asking me why I had been in Mexico and waving me through. A few feet away, a dozen or so non-US citizens waited in a glass-walled room. Some stood, some sat. Some talked with officers. The moment reminded me of a question that Hayden O'Shaughnessy, a volunteer nurse from Portland, Oregon, had voiced back at the medical units. "I have the right to go back and forth across the border and so many people don't," she had said to me. "Why do I get that privilege over them?" At the time I'd thought the answer was obvious: because you are a US citizen and they are not. But now I realized the question wasn't about having the citizenship that allowed entry; it was about having the humanity that leaves no room for barriers in the first place. In my adding up, a lack of humanity is a diseased mindset.

The border wall is visible from almost any spot in the Milpa Verde neighborhood of Brownsville. On Impala Drive—most streets in Milpa Verde are named after animals that need open, unfenced spaces: Jaguar Street, Gazelle Avenue, Leopard Street—all the houses on one side of the street have backyards that end at the border wall. In other words, it's a neighborhood at high risk for wall disease.

When Dietfried Müller-Hegemann called for wall disease to be an official diagnosis, he was thinking about the effects of the physical wall. Years later, neurologists identified cells in the brain that respond specifically to borders; the presence of a wall determines when these cells fire their signals (more on this in the next chapter). Science has not yet uncovered direct links between these cells and our psychological state, but this is the connection that Müller-Hegemann proposed. Other researchers have focused on the wall system; that is, the structure itself plus all that it represents, the rhetoric surrounding it, the anxiety triggered by that rhetoric, the restriction of movement, and whatever else a person associates with the sight of a border wall. That doesn't mean that every resident of Milpa Verde is suffering from wall disease; we simply don't know the prevalence. But it does mean that this neighborhood is a good place for understanding the symptoms people living at the border experience as part of their everyday lives.

Impala Drive doesn't look especially healthy. Most of the front yards are behind padlocked chain-link fences, making it nearly impossible to ring a doorbell. KEEP OUT, NO TRESPASSING, and BEWARE OF DOG signs also line the front yards. And there are plenty of dogs to beware of. Every house seemed to break out in a blare of barking as I walked past. The modest houses don't feel neglected. Many have gardens and decorations. Some are painted in bright colors. But there's nothing collective going on: no children in the street, no neighbors chatting. Cars speed down Impala Drive as if it were a highway and not a residential street where children might be playing. And at the edge of it all, the steel slats of the border fence interrupt the view.

Nancy Pacheco has been living in Milpa Verde for twenty-two years. She's a Texas native, but when we started talking, she asked me if I spoke Spanish (I don't) and her accent was thick enough that I had trouble understanding her. I asked if the fence made her feel safer. "Oh yes," she said. She used to be worried about people jumping the fence, but she said that the crossing stopped after the president suggested that people should be shot in the river if they tried to enter the US illegally. She was afraid of the people who crossed the border in Milpa Verde because, she said, they were drug dealers. Now, she said, the neighborhood was safe.

Her response was puzzling. The US Drug Enforcement Administration has noted that narcotics come into the United States mainly through legal ports of entry, not via people sneaking past the border.[16] Most of the drugs smuggled into the country by Joaquín Guzmán Loera, better known as El Chapo, came through legal checkpoints; so did the vast majority of heroin, cocaine, methamphetamine, and fentanyl seized at the border in 2018, according to US Customs and Border Protection.[17] Nothing adverse had ever happened to Pacheco with regard to people crossing the border in Milpa Verde. So why was she scared? I wondered if she'd always been scared, or if the locked fences had her convinced that she used to be unsafe but now she wasn't. Or if the political rhetoric surrounding the wall had led her to believe she had something to worry about. Was she genuinely concerned for her safety, or had the border wall and its backers left her paranoid and suspicious? Despite her insistence that Milpa Verde is safe, and the fact that we met in broad daylight, she kept her front gate locked as we talked.

The family a few houses over told a different story. Ruth Alejos grew up in the house she now shares with her daughter and mother. The levee where the border wall sits now was an open field when Alejos was a child. It was her backyard, up a gentle slope that begins a few feet from her back door. "We grew up on the levee," she told me. "We used to play up there." As children, she and her siblings used to slide down the slope on pieces of cardboard. Her father had a garden on the levee. They kept chickens there. An uncle of her father's was buried in a cemetery there. "It was part of us," she said.

When the family took walks up there, Border Patrol would say hi to them. The wall entirely blocks her family's access to this field, restricting their open space to the few feet of grass immediately behind their home.

Alejos, thirty-nine, used to see people crossing into the country when she was growing up, but her family never saw the need for a front gate back then. The travelers didn't worry them. She remembers some people hiding by her house when she was nine or ten years old and her mother turning on the hose so they could drink some water. "It doesn't matter where they come from if a person is thirsty." She said she hadn't seen anyone coming over the border recently, but she sometimes hears gunshots. The thought of people crossing through her yard worries her, but she's more concerned about robberies being committed by people living at the end of her street. She said she feels trapped by the wall. She wants her daughter, who is seven, to experience the joy of sliding down the levee on a piece of cardboard.

At the corner of Impala and Gazelle, Juan Rodriguez, forty-five, sat in a plastic chair in his concrete front yard behind a chain-link fence that he rolls open and closed each day. Behind him, his son jumped on a trampoline inside a net. Rodriguez, who speaks broken English, said he has given water to undocumented immigrants passing by his house. "It's OK," he said, "it's a human." He told me that the reason for the locked fences is that everyone in the neighborhood has been told that it's against the law to allow an undocumented immigrant on their property. But Rodriguez finds living behind a locked fence to be sad. "You stay in jail in your house," said Rodriguez, who came over from Mexico when he was nineteen and now works thirty hours a week delivering tortillas for nine dollars an hour. Rodriguez said he feels under surveillance and isolated from his neighbors. Border Patrol told him he needed to change a solid strip of fence to the chain-link style because it obstructed their view from one street to another. A friend who is undocumented won't visit him anymore because she's afraid of coming to the neighborhood. The Jehovah's Witnesses' Kingdom Hall across the street from him closed for the same reason: The members started feeling unsafe in Milpa Verde because Border Patrol used to go inside the church. Rodriguez said he and his wife think about leaving the neighborhood but they can't sell their house, which they put on the market not long ago for fifty-five thousand dollars, just fifteen thousand more than what he paid ten years ago, before fixing it up.

Milpa Verde is a very far cry from communist East Germany. The fear, the oppression, the danger, and the restrictions that permeated life behind the Iron Curtain are not what these residents now face. And yet the roots of wall disease are there—the fear, the isolation, the sense of immobility, the financial insecurity, the belief that people over the fence are "the other." Several people in Milpa Verde told me that they don't even notice the wall, that it's just part of the scenery. That kind of familiarity may be unavoidable. But just because we stop noticing something doesn't mean it stops affecting us.

I drove down Impala Drive on my way out of the neighborhood. The setting sun sent its last shards of brightness for the day through bollards that marked the southern border of America. I hesitated to drive through a gap in the wall, uncertain whether I had permission to be on the other side—but it was just another passageway within the US. Then I stopped at a nearby bakery selling the best Mexican sweet bread that I had ever tasted.

2

The Wall in the Brain

What Happens When We See a Border

DATO VANISHVILI IS STUCK on the wrong side of a fence. The fence has two kinds of wires. One has razor blades every few inches and the other has barbs. They are wound together like a stretched-out Slinky. Both of them are intended to rip his flesh apart should he make the mistake of trying to cross the border.

Vanishvili, eighty-six, lives in South Ossetia, a disputed territory in northern Georgia, in Eastern Europe. He came to live there only recently—but not by choice. In fact, he didn't even move there. Rather, the country changed around him, transforming from Georgia to South Ossetia at the twist of some wire. The fence, installed by the Russian government in 2013, moved his home in the Georgian village of Khurvaleti to the other side of the border with South Ossetia. Now, Vanishvili lives in a different country from the one where he made his home for eighty years, caught in the middle of a power grab in which he has no stake or interest. He cannot visit the graves of his family. He cannot go to the bank to get his pension funds. He has no way to earn money. Sometimes, Georgian police pass him loaves of bread through the two-foot-deep wire that keeps him out of his homeland. It's a kindness that helps keep him going. He refuses to leave the house he built with his own two hands. "I will never leave Georgia," he told VICE reporter Simon Ostrovsky in 2015.[1] "They can kill me, they can hang me if they like." But the truth is, he has already left and will likely never return.

The border fence between Georgia and South Ossetia is a quieter but still destructive phase of a conflict with no end in sight. Ossetians are a different ethnicity from Georgians, and the region of South Ossetia was marked off as a distinct territory within Georgia, but not a separate country, after the fall of the Soviet Union. And, for a time, everyone got along just fine—celebrating holidays together, intermarrying, and generally being neighborly with one another. But ethnic differences are ripe for exploitation. Russia stood to benefit from a conflict between South Ossetia and Georgia by, for example, giving itself geographical control over the Baku-Supsa pipeline and long stretches of Georgia's major highway. And so it began supporting separatists in South Ossetia, in a conflict that eventually culminated in a five-day war in 2008 that caused enormous suffering and destruction—reports of the damage included dead and wounded soldiers, bombed buildings, abduction, looting, revenge killings, and arson. Human Rights Watch called it "a disaster for civilians." Afterward, Russia declared its recognition of South Ossetia as a country, along with Abkhazia, another ethnically distinct region of Georgia. (Georgians do not recognize either region as an independent state and do not use the name South Ossetia.[2] Only five sovereign countries recognize South Ossetia as its own state.[3])

Then "borderization," a term used specifically for this region, began. Russian soldiers began installing fences and signs marking the line between Georgia and South Ossetia. "They put these barriers wherever they want, whenever they want," says documentary photographer Tako Robakidze, who spoke to me from her home in Georgia while on lockdown with her husband and three-month-old during the coronavirus pandemic. "People living nearby the so-called border, they live in constant fear." Border guards, whom the Russians call peacekeepers, Robakidze says, may detain anyone veering too close to the start of South Ossetia, taking them to prison in Tskhinvali, the main city in the disputed region, and demanding a few thousand rubles for release, money that people living close to the border, impoverished as a result of having their land pulled out from under them, can hardly afford. "They have no work," says Robakidze. She says that no one knows what map the Russians are using to draw the border, making the fences impossible to contest.

For Vanishvili, the border fence has affected more than his livelihood, his emotional well-being, and, potentially, his nationality. It's also changed his brain. The same goes for anyone living near a border wall, fence, sign, or other such marker. Structures like border walls alter the brain in ways that scientists are just beginning to understand.

The scientific understanding of how our brains process our geographic location began with peculiar cases of blindness. In 1909, a Hungarian neurologist named Rezsö Bálint published a case study about a patient who could see only one object at a time. Regardless of the size, regardless of how many objects were actually set before him, the patient could see just one. Bálint had never seen such a phenomenon before.[4] The patient could see each object in a scene individually but could not conceive of the scene as a whole. Even after several years of studying the patient, Bálint was at a loss to explain the strange problem. After the patient's death, an autopsy revealed brain damage to the parietal lobe, a region at the center of the brain that handles sensory information like heat and pain, and the occipital lobe, at the back, responsible for vision.

Ten years later, Gordon Holmes, a British physician who had served as a consulting neurologist on the French battlefield during World War I,[5] spoke about a patient he called J at a lecture at Trinity College, in Dublin, Ireland. J had been knocked unconscious after a shell fragment broke through his steel helmet and penetrated his skull in April 1918.[6] His eyesight was off when he came to, but the problem quickly resolved. Three weeks later, however, he began going blind, though only partially. By five weeks after the injury, he couldn't recognize red or green objects in the lower areas of his visual field. Another patient, hit by a shell fragment in October 1918, told Holmes that he couldn't find the first letters of long words or the beginnings of paragraphs. He couldn't see people right in front of him when he walked down the street. A corporal wounded that same month saw black spots for months afterward. The list went on. In all cases, damage to the parietal lobe—a region of the brain, that is, not the eye—was linked to some kind of visual impairment. These cases would eventually supply the first clues to how our brains navigate the world we move through; they indicated that sight does not depend solely on the eyes but also the brain: We have some inner mechanism for seeing the world around us.

Although these cases clearly pointed to a structure in our brains governing sight, scientists still had no idea how we navigated the world around us. Then came patient HM. In 1953, HM, an American later identified as Henry Molaison, had several portions of his brain removed to treat his severe epilepsy. The surgery ended his seizures but left him unable to form new memories of his daily life or to recall previous personal memories. As Suzanne Corkin, who observed Molaison over several years when she was a medical student, described it in her book about him[7]: "He . . . could not recall anything that relied on personal experience, such as a specific Christmas gift his father had given him. He retained only the gist of personally experienced events, plain facts, but no recollection of specific episodes."[8]

Patient HM inspired neuroscientist John O'Keefe to study memory in the late 1960s, and he began by examining single brain cells in rats. His lab had just developed a method for using electrodes to examine brain activity at this detailed level, and one day he mistakenly placed the electrodes in the wrong part of a rat's brain—the hippocampus instead of the thalamus. The error was revelatory. The cell, O'Keefe noticed, was activated in keeping with how fast the rat moved its head, or other variable behavior related to movement. He couldn't fathom why a cell triggered by movement would be located in the hippocampus, which governs memory. But the link was undeniable, and so intriguing to O'Keefe that he abruptly shifted the focus of his research to studying single brain cells tied to memory, hoping eventually to uncover how humans store and retrieve memories.[9]

But the months of research that followed led to an entirely unexpected discovery. O'Keefe and one of his students noticed that these cells, along with another type they'd found in the hippocampus, were actually firing not in response to the rat's particular motion or activity but rather in response to where the rat was in its environment at that moment. "The cells were coding for the animal's location!" O'Keefe said in his 2014 lecture when he and neuroscientists May-Britt Moser and Edvard Moser were awarded the Nobel Prize for discovering a spatial map in the brain. The hippocampus contained a navigational system using the cells O'Keefe had stumbled upon. The researchers weren't the first to conceive of the notion that animal brains contain maps; behavioral psychologist E. C. Tolman had written about it in 1948. But for the first time, science had proof that such a map existed and the names of its chief cartographers: place cells and grid cells.[10]

In the mid-1980s, James Ranck, a physiologist researching brain cells at SUNY Downstate Medical Center, in Brooklyn, New York, found yet another mental mapmaker. In a 1984 meeting of neuroscientists, Ranck played a video showing cells that fired only when an animal faced a particular direction. These head-direction cells, as Ranck called them, were proof that the brain had not only a map but also

a compass. Next came grid cells, which provide the brain
with a coordinate system, roughly analogous to our latitude
and longitude.

One more type of cell, discovered in 2008, completed the
cognitive map system. These cells, researchers found, fire at
walls. They map the enclosures of whatever environment an
animal is in. They activate when an animal is heading for
a barrier. They record the end of the line, the do-not-cross,
cannot-cross boundary. They are called border cells.

The research of cognitive map cells is still young, and neuroscientists are just beginning to understand the inner work-
ings and significance of all these mechanisms. But enough
evidence has accumulated to affirm the importance of each
component. Border cells are fewer in number than grid cells,
but they are crucial for creating an accurate mental representation of the environment. Simply, border cells tell us where
the boundaries are. They activate only in the presence of wall-
like edges, and their presence indicates just how important
borders are in determining our location.[11] If a wall is erected
where none stood before, the border cells reconfigure to fire
at the right moment. They warn the animal that movement
stops here.

Although research of the cognitive map has been confined
to animals thus far, scientists believe the same system exists
in humans. The purpose of border cells, says Edvard Moser,
is to help an animal align with its surroundings. These cells
may fire at the presence of a cliff or a long stone—anything
straight that stands out from the background can enable an
animal to orient itself, says Moser.

After the discovery of border cells, Moser wanted to know whether they reacted to border structures solely as a sensory cue—the structure is there, so the cells fire—or if the presence of a border structure conveyed some other information about the environment. His lab conducted an experiment in which a wall inside a box containing a mouse was lifted a tiny bit, just enough for the mouse to creep under. When the wall was raised, the border cells stopped firing, even though the structure was still in the box. Before it was raised, the wall had been integrated into the mouse's cognitive map not just because it was there as a structure but because it indicated a no-go area. As soon as the mouse could move past it, the wall no longer mattered.

The practical need for a navigation system in the brain is obvious. We need to go places and it helps not to have to figure out how to get to those places every time we have to run some errands or drop off a child at a friend's house. Thus the connection to the hippocampus, the seat of memory, makes sense. And if road construction blocks a route for a few weeks, we need to remember that this blockade exists so we follow an alternate path. Our memory of our environment is wired for changes like this, says Moser. "Because of that, the human species and all mammals are very good at surviving," he says. "It's an enormous advantage."

The brain of a person living near a border wall contains cells that fire every time the wall is in view. If the person grew up in the shadow of the structure, then it has always been part of their cognitive map. If the structure was added to the environment later, then the person's map adapted to include it. If a border wall is in your midst, then it's in your cognitive map.

That connection seems intuitive and also sensible from the perspective of survival. We are hardwired to remember our surroundings. But although the science of spatial maps is still young, there are reasons to suspect that there is more to the story. Namely, the spatial map is very likely connected to our emotions. "When we create a map of our environment, it is rarely a purely physical map," says Moser. "Elements of the map also depend on how important they are to us emotionally." The security fence in Jerusalem, which evokes feelings on both sides, is an example of how a place in our mental maps becomes linked to our emotions, says Moser. Some Palestinians refer to it as the apartheid wall, and some Israelis call it an anti-terror fence; either way, the structure is tightly knitted to an emotional response.[12] Or take 9/11. People remember where they were when the planes hit the Twin Towers in 2001 because the moment was so significant. "Spatial representation in the hippocampus is most likely influenced by emotions," says neuroscientist Gabrielle Girardeau, of France's National Institute for Health and Medical Research (INSERM). We may not remember what we had for lunch last week, but we will remember the restaurant where we got dumped.

The link between emotions and cognitive maps likely has roots in survival. The appearance of a predator at a certain spot must be remembered in order to avoid that spot in the future, explains Girardeau. A jolt of fear may accompany the next crossing. On the flip side, it helps to have a good emotional connection to a place that is safe or bountiful. "Very simply," says Girardeau, "you have to remember what bad things and good things happened, where to avoid them, and where to look for them."

That seems straightforward enough for a prey animal trying to live through the night in the savanna. But the link between the cognitive map and the emotions becomes potentially more fraught when it's taking place in humans. Girardeau sees a possible connection to post-traumatic stress disorder, which is typically linked to discrete events. For someone like Dato Vanishvili, the trauma of the fence may then be reinforced every time he sees it. "It's almost like classical conditioning, like Pavlov's dog," says Moser. "You see something that evokes strong emotions, and each time you see it, that emotion comes up."

The border fence has been nothing but traumatic for Vanishvili. Of the eighty Georgian families that lived near him, only he and his grandson remain. The threat of harm pervades their days. "Ossetians told my grandson that if he tried to cross the border, they will catch him, take him to Russia and throw him in jail," Vanishvili told *Arab News* in 2018.[13] Yet on the other side of the fence from his homeland, he is already a prisoner. He cannot visit his daughters.[14] He cannot walk his fields as he's done for so many years, because they are now on the other side of the fence. He says that guards are watching him, and the Russian government will seize his home if he crosses into Georgia. "I don't have food, bread, I don't have anything," he told CNN in 2017, from behind the tangle of barbed wire that now filters his view of

his surroundings.[15] "What should I do, kill myself?" The concertina wire marking the edge of his homeland triggers Vanishvili's border cells to fire every time he sees it, and in turn,
that firing may trigger the despair associated with that place.

Sometimes the emotional effect may be subtler.
Claus-Christian Carbon, a psychologist at the University
of Bamberg, in Germany, had repeatedly observed drivers
following the same routes they drove when the Berlin Wall
still stood, even though it now meant traveling longer than
necessary. The phenomenon made him wonder about how
the wall still shaped people's everyday thinking. In the early
2000s, he and a colleague, Helmut Leder, turned their attention to cognitive maps. Do feelings that aren't born from
traumatic events still shape our view of the physical world?
If so, would people's views of the Berlin Wall still reside in
their mental maps?

There was reason to think so. Research in the 1960s found
an inverse relationship between emotional involvement with
a city and the estimate of how far away it was. The more feelings a person had about a city, the closer that person believed
it to be. The greater the emotional involvement, the fewer
the kilometers.[16] Many years later, researchers at Texas State
University asked students about their attitudes toward Canada, the United States, and Mexico. Participants who had
positive feelings about people of other races, nationalities,
and ethnicities estimated cities in Mexico and Canada as being closer than those who held negative or neutral feelings.

Carbon and Leder wanted to know whether the same
pattern held true in the relationship between Germans and

places in their own country. They asked eighty-three people, some of whom had been raised in the former East Germany and some in the former West Germany, to estimate the distance between cities situated in these areas, and also asked about their attitude toward reunification. By majority, those who held a negative view of reunification tended to estimate cities that used to be on the opposite sides of the wall as farther apart than they actually were. The same overestimating did not happen for cities that had been on the same side of the wall. And people with a positive attitude about reunification did not overestimate the distances. "There still exists a mental gap between East and West—even in young people—fifteen years after the German reunification," Carbon and Leder wrote in their 2005 paper.[17] They named the phenomenon the "mental wall."

Carbon revisited the data a few years later because he wanted to know how the participants were gauging distance. Were they estimating the distance between cities "as the crow flies," or were they thinking about how long a drive it was on the Autobahn? The results of this additional study found it to be the latter; participants were picturing the drive from place to place. That detail was important, because it meant they were using their cognitive maps, mental images based on their own experience. The finding, says Carbon, shows just how much our emotional life shapes our view of the world.

Our maps of the world are skewed by many emotions and thought patterns. Researchers from China found that people estimate cities that share a dialect to be closer than cities that do not.[18] We tend to associate north with up and up with good—and south with down and bad; the north-facing world map we are accustomed to elicits a bias that the northern parts of the world are somehow better than the southern parts.[19] That bias vanishes when the map is presented "upside down"—that is, with the Southern Hemisphere at the top, the Pacific Ocean at the center, and the Atlantic Ocean split in two. At the same time, studies have found that people think traveling north takes longer than traveling south. The fact that our sense of geography is colored by our biases is evidence of some connection between the cognitive map cells and the emotional regions of the brain.

In another experiment, Carbon asked 220 volunteers at the University of Vienna about their attitude toward the war between the US and Iraq, which was still ongoing at the time of the study, and their attitude toward US citizens. Then he asked the participants to estimate the distances between six cities in Europe, six in the US, and Baghdad, Iraq. The results were more complex than earlier studies but reinforce the notion that we bias our cognitive maps with our emotions. Participants who disliked Americans estimated cities across the ocean as farther away when they also felt negatively toward the war. But participants who liked Americans also overestimated distances to cities across the Atlantic when they felt favorably toward the war. Carbon reasoned that people who identify with the US—they liked Americans and the war—would see European cities as farther away because of that emotional involvement, as if they were seeing the world through American eyes.

In other words, border walls aren't just border walls. Any place where we have a noteworthy experience becomes tinged with emotion. Kate Jeffery, a neuroscientist at University College London, explains that the amygdala— the emotional center of the brain—plays a role in spatial awareness by sending messages like, *This is a place where bad things happen.* A border wall, says Jeffery, is a place of complex understandings, including social hierarchies and the ability to separate friends from enemies. And so, we end up with an endless loop. The border wall is tied to an emotion stemming from our experience of that place, and we reconnect to that emotion every time we see it by virtue of the connection between the cognitive map and our emotions.

Not everyone in the shadow of a border wall has strong feelings about it. Israel Yañez, the security guard at Ross clothing store in Brownsville, was nonplussed about the sight of the border wall. In Milpa Verde, Maria Santos, fifty-two, who had emigrated from Mexico and now had to stare at a wall in her backyard that was put there for the sole purpose of stopping others from achieving the same goal told me, in Spanish (translated by her daughter), that she really didn't think much about the wall at all.

Maybe the very different experiences that Santos and Vanishvili had at their respective borders resulted in very different emotional ties to their cognitive maps of their respective border walls. Santos had the life for which she'd come to America, at least to some extent. Vanishvili had everything taken away from him. And increasingly, it's experiences like Vanishvili's—and their resultant pain—that are being replicated at border walls around the world.

Scientists are just beginning to understand the cells that make up our cognitive maps, along with whether, and how, this system interacts with emotional regions of the brain. But we know enough to suspect a connection. When the physical environment changes, so do the map cells, reconfiguring in order to keep us away from danger and on paths that contribute to our survival. "Emotions influence this representation," says Girardeau. And copious evidence points to the role emotions play in biasing our sense of distance, our estimation of how easy a place is to access, and our assessment of how desirable that destination is. So there is solid reason to think that border walls not only reshape our brain but do so in a way that is entangled with whatever emotions the wall triggers. For people living in borderlands, those emotions are often negative.

3

The Other Side of the Border

How Walls Create "the Other"

ON APRIL 5, 2017, a model S2R-T34 Turbo Thrush aircraft flew along the border between Israel and the Palestinian territories near the city of Khan Yunis, in the southern Gaza Strip. It dove low several times and sprayed glyphosate, oxyfluorfen, and diuron in long lines parallel to the border. Glyphosate is also known as Roundup. The spray was an herbicidal mix intended to kill vegetation so that desert weeds would not obscure the view from Israel into the occupied region.

The Israeli military directs pilots to spray herbicide only on an easterly wind. Distant smoke from a burning tire shows the pilots the wind direction to ensure that the herbicide blows onto the borderline but not farther into Gaza. But, as later crop damage would show, the chemicals likely blew far beyond the border they were intended to treat. "By God," a man standing in a field a few hundred meters from the border said as he shot a video of the flight with his phone. "We know not from where we receive these troubles."[1] The wind was strong enough to carry droplets of herbicide about three hundred meters past the border, straight into growing fields in the Gaza Strip. Sickly white spots soon dotted the leaves of chard and spinach that had been nearly ready for the spring harvest. Zucchini and pea plants showed the same damage. "You have to understand this in the context of food security," says Samaneh Moafi, a researcher with Forensic Architecture, a research agency based at Goldsmiths, University of London that investigated the spraying, "and how precious it is for Gazan farmers to produce their own food."

A border wall can change our brain, triggering new neurological signals and reconfiguring our mental maps, possibly influenced by our emotional experiences of the wall. But the stress and insecurity stemming from border walls may cause even more dramatic alterations to our mental health. The extreme anxiety triggered by crop destruction—nothing to harvest means no money or nothing to eat—is one stark example, but others abound across the globe. For many Israelis, the same wall connects to other painful memories just by the fact of being a wall. Eli Somer, professor emeritus of psychology at the University of Haifa in Israel, says of Holocaust survivors: "They know about being fenced in." It's not just the wall but what it represents. It's the wall system that matters, Cornell sociologist Christine Leuenberger and others emphasize—the politics, the rationale, the history, and the attitudes that are mixed into the concrete and threaded through the barbed wire.

Border walls are nothing new. Cities have walled themselves off from their surroundings for thousands of years. The Sumerian king Gilgamesh inscribed his heroic acts on the walls circling the ancient city of Uruk a few thousand years ago.² Chariots raced along the tops of the forty-foot-high walls built by Nebuchadnezzar II around Babylon in the sixth century BCE. Walls have long marked the edges of fortresses and palaces. For as long as humans have wanted to keep one another out, walls—a word deriving from the Latin *vallus* for "stake" or "post"—have been erected.

The first known wall intended to mark a land boundary stood in Ur, located in what is now Iraq, built by the Sumerian king Shulgi around 2038 BCE. This 155-mile barrier, which spanned the distance between the Tigris and Euphrates Rivers, was supposed to block the Amorites, a seminomadic people inhabiting the area once known as Canaan. The problem with the wall was that it had ends. The Amorites, driven to invade the Sumerian kingdom, possibly owing to drought in the Middle East, simply walked around it. Their attack contributed to the collapse of the Sumerian civilization.³ Construction of the Great Wall of China began about 1,800 years later, though the structure that stands today is largely the creation of the seventeenth-century Ming dynasty,⁴ which ended when Manchurian invaders overcame the dynasty's defense at the Shanghai Pass, on the eastern end of the wall. More recently, China used the wall to control immigration. Numerous other examples still stand, many now preserved as historic monuments commemorating humanity's past efforts to protect ourselves from one another. As a biographer of the Roman emperor Hadrian supposedly wrote, the eighty miles of stone that constituted Hadrian's Wall in Roman-ruled Britain were placed "to separate the Romans from the barbarians."⁵

As ancient as border walls may be, the international boundaries they mark today derive from a European approach to parceling out the land we inhabit. The idea of distinct countries and states, each with its own economy, government, and borders—as opposed to empires, nomadic regions, dynasties, or city-states—comes from Europe, beginning in the seventeenth century and "becoming the compulsion it is today" in the nineteenth and early twentieth centuries, says John Agnew, professor of geography at the University of California, Los Angeles. Empires are more strongly bound by obedience to a ruler than by ethnic or other identity, for example. Early dynasties viewed territory in terms of family bonds rather than belonging to a singular "people." And city-states were more about trade than governing large pieces of land with homogeneous populations. In contrast to all of these, the modern nation-state revolves around nationality, providing a government that is "invested in the identities and interests of 'their' people," says Agnew. He sees the use of this Euro-American model in the modern Middle East and Africa as a political tragedy because in these regions, people of various ethnic and religious identities are spread out in ways that don't conform to sharp borders.[6] People on one side aren't always different from people on the other. Defined national borders are a way for nationalist movements and their leaders to gain control because they create differences between populations that can then be leveraged for power. "Strong spatial demarcations," says Agnew, "are particularly useful when other mechanisms for defining a group are weak."

National borders eventually necessitated the passport. Just over a hundred years ago, people could move about as they pleased. "Before 1914 the earth had belonged to all," Austrian author Stefan Zweig wrote in his 1941 memoir *The World of Yesterday.* "There were no permits, no visas, and it always gives me pleasure to astonish the young by telling them that before 1914 I traveled from Europe to India and to America without passport and without ever having seen one."[7] Travel documents did exist; the word "passport" comes from seventeenth-century France, where officials of King Louis XIV carried *passe-port* ("pass through ports") documents that let them do just that.[8] When the Industrial Revolution arrived, people began traveling abroad in droves, with minimal (if any) restriction. Anti-immigration policies, such as the US's Chinese Exclusion Act of 1882, are a stain on this otherwise liberating era. Through the early 1900s, passports did not loom large in people's minds.

World War I changed that. Spies and revolutionaries abounded, and people throughout Europe sought to move across countries. Governments began requiring travelers to show their passports in order to confirm their citizenship and identity with the goal of restricting movement across the continent.[9] The US was also concerned about an influx of immigrants, and likewise increased its passport enforcement.[10] These documents had to have basic information about the carrier as well as a photograph. Such restrictions remained in place after the battles ended, and so Europe, once easy to move through, became a new kind of minefield, paperwork replacing the artillery.[11] Many people considered passports to be dehumanizing. "The humiliations which once had been devised with criminals alone in mind now were imposed upon the traveler, before and during every journey," wrote Zweig. The League of Nations, a diplomatic group founded by several world leaders to preserve world peace following the war, had vowed to "secure and maintain freedom of communications and of transit" for all citizens whose countries belonged to the league.[12] But as it turns out, passport policies have often accomplished exactly the opposite, belonging to the same world as border walls: one that controls by limiting movement.

After the Great War, some people longed for a return to the days before passports. At a 1920 conference, the league deemed that impossible. They did, however, recognize that the documents had become unnecessarily complicated and arduous—different countries required different information—and they agreed to simplify matters by making passports the same everywhere: thirty-two pages, in French and the language of the home nation, bound in cardboard, and with space for photographs of "the bearer and his wife."[13] The document would be valid for up to two years, a fee to be paid at each renewal. At a second conference in 1925, the league again considered eradicating the "passport regime," as legal scholar Daniel Turack called it in 1968. By then that idea was already deemed too radical.[14]

Awareness of the peril some international travelers faced influenced the deliberations surrounding passports after World War II. A committee convened by the United Nations at that time forthrightly opposed, for example, the practice of governments' keeping a foreign traveler's passport for the duration of his or her stay.[15] But again, they also agreed that a world without passports was permanently past.

In 1963, representatives from eighty-seven countries traveled to Rome for the United Nations Conference on International Travel and Tourism. They made several decisions on small but significant passport details: The application procedures should be simplified; description of the bearer could be limited to height, eye color, and "special peculiarities"[16] (the 1925 version had required profession, address, and hair color). They also voiced support for article 13 of the Universal Declaration of Human Rights, which states, "Everyone has the right to leave any country, including his own, and to return to his country."[17]

Generally speaking, passports don't convey that spirit of freedom. We fear losing them when we're abroad. We keep them locked in safes in our hotel rooms, or in hard-to-see carriers tucked inside our shirts. They are precious documents because they prove our citizenship, an essential commodity should we ever be forced out of our homeland, or become separated from our children by brutal war, or wish to skip the longer waiting line at the bridge from Matamoros to Brownsville. They are also used to deny entry to countries, to determine the level of scrutiny we warrant while traveling, and to track our movements around the world. The passport, Turack wrote, "has been used as an instrument to infringe the fundamental human right of freedom of movement."

Passports provide crucial historical context for understanding border walls. They are, in a sense, a precursor to the modern border wall. As Élisabeth Vallet puts it, passports are like border walls that we carry around. The Universal Declaration of Human Rights states that everyone has the right to leave and return to their country, but in reality they can do so only with a passport. They force us to internalize the boundaries imposed on us. And like border walls, their power lies not just in the paper but in the system surrounding it—the rhetoric and restrictions and the ensuing sense of oppression, fear, and anxiety. Above all, the history of passports clarifies the fact that the restrictions on movement between countries are a recent phenomenon. Life wasn't always like this. Passports and border walls are artificial, and as any nutritionist will tell us, artificial is where the trouble starts.

India and Pakistan gained independence from Great Britain in 1947. Between them, set among the western Himalayas and the Karakoram Mountains, the land known as Kashmir sat like a piece of gold. Initially independent, too, Kashmir immediately found itself under invasion by Pakistani tribes[18] and under pressure by the Muslim majority in the monarch-ruled state, who opposed the maharaja. So the government decided to give the nation to India in return for protection. India and Pakistan have been fighting over this region, which is about the size of Kansas, ever since. Today, Kashmir, now often referred to as Jammu and Kashmir, is split between the two countries, with a small northwest portion under Chinese rule. Glacial and fresh water that generate electricity and irrigate crops for billions of people make the region desirable and thus a source of bitter conflict[19]— one sure to worsen as climate change brings drought to nearby regions. Three wars over the past seventy years have left death and destruction on both sides. And they've left people living in borderland villages tormented by several dangers. Just sympathizing or fraternizing with people across the border can be seen as a crime.

For the people of Kashmir, the five-hundred-mile border separating India's area from Pakistan's, known as the Line of Control, is random. Families on either side share ancestry, religion, and ethnicity.[20] Like South Ossetians and Georgians, they once shared their lives. The border put a halt to that. "Overnight our identity changed from being a mainlander of Kashmir to a borderlander in Kashmir," someone living near the Line of Control told Debidatta Mahapatra, who directs the Mahatma Gandhi Center for Nonviolence, Human Rights, and World Peace at the Hindu University of America. "We became Indian citizens and those who happened to be on the other side of the border became Pakistanis."[21]

A new nationality had been forced upon them, and border residents had to demonstrate their allegiance to the side they were on. "Cross-border connections, even emotional ones, were deemed anti-national," Mahapatra wrote in 2016. Villagers near the Line of Control denied connections with anyone on the other side. But no matter how much they voiced their loyalty—an insistence driven largely by fear— authorities still viewed them with suspicion, says Mahapatra. The Line of Control scissored through villages, forcing the creation of "the other," an artificial divide between humans who had never seen themselves as different.

The othering of people is one of the strongest weapons that those who favor border walls have. Nationalism depends on the belief that the people on the other side of the fence are not only different but also inferior and threatening. Russia exploits ethnic pride among South Ossetians in its ploy to gain control of Georgian territory,[22] using a fence of barbed and razor wire to create division.[23] The more the Ossetians view Georgians as "the other," the more successful Russia will be. As long as citizens view people across a border as a threat, politicians will gain political clout through wall building—which of course means that politicians have an incentive to fuel that perception.

Othering isn't just for nationalists. The Cutteslowe walls, built in 1934, separated middle-class homeowners from public housing renters in Oxford, England[24]; that was their purpose. The walls separated the poorer residents from the wealthier ones. "It had nothing to do with race or ethnicity," says Agnew. "They were worried about their property values." Gated communities, especially in well-to-do neighborhoods, often carry the same implications: Those on the outside are different from those on the inside.

Sometimes, othering makes us want what's on the other side. The Prussian king Frederick the Great, who ruled in the 1700s, understood a thing or two about walls. He had ordered his subjects to grow potatoes, which had been introduced to Europe by the Spanish in the 1500s. He believed potatoes would prevent famine and make bread cheaper. European farmers distrusted this unfamiliar root vegetable. "What the peasant doesn't know he will not eat," went a saying of the time. One town flat-out refused the king's order. Potatoes, they told their monarch, "have neither smell nor taste, not even the dogs will eat them, so what use are they to us?"

And so, the story goes, Frederick built a wall, of sorts. He told his public that soldiers would be vigilantly guarding the potato fields he'd cultivated near Berlin, Prussia's first. Secretly, though, he told the army not to guard too heavily. Maybe, he told them, they could pretend to fall asleep now and then, and then pretend not to wake up if someone entered the field to steal a potato, which is exactly what happened. Frederick knew that putting potatoes behind a barrier would make people want them, a thing he could not achieve by command. They wanted what was on the other side because the wall (of soldiers, in this case) had made what was on the inside seem better than what was on the outside.[25]

The modern border wall isn't there to entice people over to the other side. But that is one of its effects. Often, those enticements are real: jobs, safety, a different future for one's children. Even when those visions are just chimeras, though, the wall tantalizes. Refugees living in tents on a dusty hillside at the northern edge of Mexico believe they will find a better life on the other side. The border wall that keeps them from pursuing that dream doesn't quell their desire to do so; just the opposite. Gated communities play similar games with our emotions, making what's on the other side simultaneously desirable and out of reach.

European farmers ultimately embraced the potato, pushed to some extent by the want instilled in them by the barrier. But with borders, that want ricochets off the wall and morphs into shame and humiliation. In Lima, Peru, a tall concrete barrier separates rich from poor through six miles of the city. People living in the regions on the poor side often call it El Muro de la Vergüenza, the Wall of Shame. A Jesuit college was the first private institution in Lima to build a barrier around itself. Wealthy residents soon followed suit, building the wall over thirty years.[26] Many children in Lima have never been on the other side of the wall and have no idea what's there. Poor workers must spend hours traveling to jobs on the other side of the wall that are really just a short distance away. In Las Casuarinas, on the rich side, mansion balconies overlook manicured lawns and swimming pools.[27] In Pamplona Alta, on the poor side, rectangular shacks made of wood and corrugated metal sit like steps on a mountain. The area has run out of room for building. There is no running water or sewage system. Shredded plastic bags hang on the barbed wire atop the concrete wall, which is patrolled day and night. "It's the physical manifestation of a symbolic problem," Peruvian photographer Roberto Huarcaya says in a 2018 documentary by European television producer ARTE. "I think each of us in Peru carries a wall within us."

Othering at a country level oppresses entire ethnicities and nationalities and foments dangerous ideals like white supremacy that lead to violence and insecurity. "Division drives fear and fear drives populism, and populism drives authoritarianism," says Vallet, who was the first person to report just how many border walls there now are across the world.

Hungary is a case in point. The Austro-Hungarian Empire was carved up into Romania, Hungary, Czechoslovakia, and the former Yugoslavia by the Treaty of Trianon following World War I. Poland also regained the portion of its land that had been consumed by the empire. The treaty shrank Hungary by about two thirds and placed one third of ethnic Hungarians in the newly created countries just outside their homeland's borders. For decades, Hungarians maintained that their nation extended beyond the borders drawn on modern maps.

Then 2015 arrived, and with it an influx of refugees into the European Union. Hungary's location between the Middle East and Western Europe prompted the Hungarian government to build a fence at its border with Serbia,[28] a border it had fought since its inception. "For me, the puzzle was, how is it possible to think of those people and territories outside the border as part of your nation and at the same time, to build a wall between you and them?" says Gela Merabishvili, a graduate student in political geography at Virginia Tech. Before 2015, says Merabishvili, who is Hungarian and currently living there, the borders were "painful memories of the dismemberment of Hungary." He says people often used language like that, of a body being mutilated. But once the refugees arrived, a fence was built on that very line.

Merabishvili believes that the presence of the fence brought fear of the refugees. Many Hungarians were initially fine with allowing them to pass through their country. But whatever ambivalence existed was fueled by reports on Hungarian state-controlled television linking terrorism with immigration. "People started to fear more and more," says Merabishvili, "and the government started to adopt more militaristic language and practices." Anyone crossing the border illegally, for example, could be sent to prison for years.[29] In September 2015, Hungarian riot police launched tear gas at a crowd that had broken through one of the razor wire fences separating them from entry into the country from Serbia.

"The fence is a powerful stage," writes Annastiina Kallius, a social anthropology researcher at the University of Helsinki, "a set for the government's incessant antimigrant, Islamophobic campaigns waged ever since the 2015 attack on the offices of the satirical newspaper *Charlie Hebdo* in Paris."[30] And the more the government portrayed the refugees as a population to fear—driven, in part, by competition with a far-right political party espousing nationalistic views—the more its citizens did so. "They deprived their opponent of their main ammunition," says Merabishvili, "which was this radical vocabulary." The refugees were no longer humans seeking safety from war and deprivation in Syria. They had become "the other."

A similar, if less destructive, pattern is evident in Northern Ireland, where the period known as the Troubles led to the erection of "peace lines"—fences, barriers, walls, and so forth—to stop fighting between Protestant and Catholic communities. Nearly one hundred such barriers still stand in Belfast alone.[31] The peace lines are not necessarily needed to halt violence anymore. But many people want to keep them in place because they don't trust those on the other side. Although the barriers stopped the fighting between these two communities, they also became a physical expression of division.[32] The populations have changed over the years; Catholic communities grew, their average age decreasing, and Protestant communities shrank, their average age increasing. As a result, their interests compete for entirely different reasons from those that brought about the peace lines in the first place. Protestant neighborhoods fear they will lose territory if the barriers are removed because of their shrinking populations. Older Protestants worry about rowdy Catholic teenagers. By contrast, the nationalist parties, which represent the Catholic working class, see evidence of discrimination and deprivation tied to the peace lines and the way in which these structures exacerbate differences between the two sides. "You create a single identity and community behind a wall," says Jonny Byrne, a social scientist at Ulster University, "and that's dangerous because it's an ethnic society." Each side ends up with a lack of diversity and false views of the other side that make building a cohesive community, sans peace lines, extremely difficult.

These ideas resonate with people, says Gerard Toal, professor of government and international affairs at Virginia Tech, and Merabishvili's mentor, "because of deeply held notions about identity and homeland." Toal sees the nationalistic rhetoric surrounding border walls as a sort of performance based around a metaphysical threat. Dramatic global shifts such as climate change, which is resculpting the planet, and coronavirus only reinforce the appeal of finding safety in one's nation, says Toal, which means the rhetoric will likely continue to increase. The horror of this reality is used to justify the continued promotion of border walls.

The othering of people across a border explains Claus-Christian Carbon's findings about the tendency of Germans to overestimate distances between cities on opposite sides of the former Berlin Wall. It explains why people in Brownsville, Texas, don't always identify with asylum seekers in the tent camp just over the border in Matamoros, even though so many of them trace their heritage to Mexico. It explains why Israel might turn a blind eye to the destruction of crops in the Gaza Strip. "The other has become invisible and unseen," says Gilad Hirschberger, professor of psychology at IDC Herzliya, a private research college in Israel.

Of course none of these pictures are complete. All of these situations have nuances, difficult histories, and complexities beyond the scope of this book. A border wall may offer a necessary security measure in the short term. But the psychological toll of living near these structures is often rooted in the view that humans on one side are different from those on the other. Both sides bear the consequences.

4

Mortal Danger

The Fear of Living Near a Border Wall

FELANI KHATUN AND HER FATHER arrived at the fence separating India from Bangladesh on January 7, 2011, at about eight thirty in the morning. They'd been traveling all night with the help of a smuggler and had finally reached the Anantapur border in the Cooch Behar district of northern India. Felani, fifteen, was the Indian-born daughter of migrant workers from Bangladesh, and she and her father were returning to their homeland so she could be married. They had wanted to arrive when it was still dark out and now had to risk climbing the fence in the light of day. The young girl stood out against the gray sky in her dress of red and royal blue. A ladder propped up against the fence was all that separated the father and daughter from their destination. Felani's father climbed over without a problem. But her dress caught on the barbs, and when she screamed for help a member of India's Border Security Force shot her in the chest.[1]

Felani's body remained on the fence for the next five hours. One leg lay horizontally across the top of the fence and the other was slung over the side, dangling into India. The top half of her body hung upside down, her ponytail still tidy, her necklace fallen around her chin, a heart-shaped charm hovering by her forehead. Border officers stood a few feet away. People nearby said they heard her begging for water while she died. Eventually the border patrol tied her ankles and wrists onto a bamboo pole and carried her body away. The officer who allegedly shot her was acquitted twice.[2]

The border fence between India and Bangladesh is known as the bloodiest in the world.[3] Between 2000 and 2010, the Border Security Force killed nearly one thousand people, mostly Bangladeshis, according to Human Rights Watch.[4] Some of the victims were not even trying to cross over the fence. This border is far from the only dangerous one worldwide. The terrorist group Boko Haram unleashed its nightmare of abduction, killing, and conscription near the border of Chad and Niger.[5] Land mines dot the demilitarized zone between North Korea and South Korea,[6] and anyone who tries to cross the border may be shot.[7] MORTAL DANGER, reads a sign on the separation barrier between Israel and the Palestinian territories.[8] ANY PERSON WHO PASSES OR DAMAGES THIS FENCE ENDANGERS HIS LIFE.

The wall itself may not always be particularly frightening; the bollards separating Brownsville from Matamoros may stop migrants but they won't tear your flesh apart. From eye level, they look a little like a fence surrounding a park for giants. Yet fear is now embedded into our collective conception of border walls. All of these structures are connected to a mindset that seeks to control us by the fear of what will happen if we attempt to breach them: death, prison, tear gas, or the command to return to a homeland drenched in violence, corruption, and deprivation.

Geographers sometimes refer to the proliferation of border walls across the world as spatial apartheid. Barriers are used to segregate populations that are deemed to be threatening, whether out of genuine concern or because instilling that belief helps ensure, say, reelection. Regardless of the underlying motive for a border wall, the structures themselves are one component—though a visible and imposing one—of a power dynamic. "The wall really symbolizes all of the enforcement that happens around it," says Reece Jones, professor of geography at the University of Hawai'i at Mānoa. The physical wall represents the system that has decided who's in and who's out, and what happens to those who try to change that equation.

Eyal Weizman, who founded Forensic Architecture, the research team that investigated the herbicide spraying at the Gaza Strip, uses starker terms. "What we are seeing is just the monster's tail," he says, "and there is something terrifyingly scary about seeing the tail of a beast whose full contours and capacity and disposition we do not yet know." Weizman was speaking not about the wall between Israel and the Gaza Strip specifically but about all border walls. Around the world, the consequences of long-term stress caused by the fear and insecurity stemming from border structures are slowly making themselves known. "The fear that walls trigger is what we should fear," says geographer Élisabeth Vallet.

For those who live and work near border walls, fear is often part of routine life. The fence between India and Bangladesh cuts through miles of rice paddies tended to by farmers daily. "It's frightening if you're just trying to go about your

life, working in your rice paddy, and you have to worry about
bullets flying past," says Jones, who wrote about this and
other borders in his book *Border Walls: Security and the War
on Terror in the United States, India, and Israel*. Many people have family on the other side, but visiting them means
bribing border guards. Halfway across the short bridge from
Matamoros into Brownsville, armed guards check passports
while standing near a stack of riot gear. In Georgia, shep-
herds who've strayed too close to the border have been im-
prisoned in Tskhinvali, South Ossetia, their families left with
no idea of when their husband, father, brother, or son might
return home. In many places, the military presence engen-
ders a sense of being watched and potentially punished for
the slightest transgression.

Somewhat harder to see is the fear triggered in people
whose government built the wall ostensibly to keep them
safe. In August 1962, Peter Fechter, an eighteen-year-old
bricklayer living on the East German side of the Berlin Wall,
which had been built a year earlier, tried to leave by climbing
over and dropping into West Berlin. The friend with whom
he'd cooked up the plan succeeded, but East German border
guards shot Fechter in his right hip. He fell onto the East
German side of the wall—where he lived—and died within
an hour. East Germans had been told that the purpose of the
Berlin Wall was to keep out Western fascists. But the truth
was that the wall was made to keep East Germans in; that
was increasingly clear. Those on the communist side of the
wall lived in fear of the very authorities who praised their
system as superior.

The current situation in the United States is not comparable. Citizens of El Paso don't worry that they may not come home if they walk into Mexico for the afternoon. But subtle cues still provoke mild fear. Vallet recounts conversations she had with immigrants in the Rio Grande Valley who told her that people don't talk to them anymore. "Everyone is shying away from them, not touching them, not looking at them," she recalls their telling her. It was as if the border wall and its accompanying rhetoric had made people treat immigrants like they had cooties, lest they be seen treating the enemy kindly. Locals urged her not to speed, to avoid drawing the attention of the police, and told her where she could and could not go. "It felt like a dystopian atmosphere," she says. "You feel under surveillance." The US-Mexico border is dotted with towers that enable Border Patrol to watch for activity in the river and at its Mexican shores, but they also provide a handy view of neighborhoods on the US side. And undocumented workers worry about being stopped on the highway, or anywhere for that matter.

Israel provides another example of a border wall that influences the minds of those it's supposed to protect. Construction of the security wall between Israel and the Palestinian territories began in 2002 as a response to the suicide bombings during the second Intifada—138 such attacks occurred between October 2000 and July 2005. (This history is long, complicated, and beyond the scope of this book.) The structure worked: These terrorist acts decreased in frequency, leaving Israelis to live without the constant fear of a deadly bomb exploding every time they went to a shopping mall or café. But the same people now protected by the wall must also live with how it affects those on the other side: cutting croplands off from their owners, transecting villages, and making movement from one area to another complicated or even impossible. "The wall creates a clear reminder that the two people are still in conflict," says Eli Somer, "and reminds us of the difficulties the other side incurs as a result of the existence of this wall." Israel also has a fence along its 150-mile border with Egypt—in order to prevent drug and weapons smuggling and illegal immigration—and a fence at the border with Jordan has been started, with plans for additional structures at the borders with Syria. "When this happens, Israel will effectively turn into an armed fortress sealing itself off from its surroundings," says the psychology professor Gilad Hirschberger. Although this situation provides a sense of psychological and physical security, he says, "it also cultivates paranoia, distrust, and perpetual existential fear."

For some people, the rhetoric surrounding the border wall has provided a useful way to redirect other fears, such as anxieties about job loss and financial insecurity. It's scapegoating at the societal level, says Daniel Sullivan, a social psychologist at the University of Arizona. Blaming groups that we aren't part of—minority groups, political parties, a particular demographic, outsiders—for uncertainties or ambiguities in our lives, says Sullivan, helps us handle those uncertainties and ambiguities.

Sullivan runs the Cultural-Existential Psychology Laboratory, where researchers conduct experiments to understand how people cope with suffering, the threat of death, and other challenging life events. In one typical study, they asked a group of adults to think about large problems, such as climate change or the 2008 recession, and to provide opinions on who could be blamed for these issues. Then, they asked them to consider the roles of specific participants, such as a particular country's contribution to climate change or a senator who may have contributed to the 2008 recession. In this case, the targets weren't entirely blameless to begin with, and the volunteers were given a chance to vent about these actors. Providing this opportunity exacerbated the scapegoating. "Basically, what we see is that if people have been threatened, they tend to blame these targets even more," says Sullivan. "People often feel, at least temporarily, a greater sense of control when they do this."

Those in power know this, says Sullivan. First comes the problem—unemployment, global warming, coronavirus. Then comes the fear-generating rhetoric—for example, calling undocumented immigrants "thugs" and "animals"[9] that are invading the country. The more convinced we are to blame these groups, the less likely we are to consider more nuanced truths about underlying causes, allowing those in power to avoid culpability. Other times, Sullivan points out, politicians may completely manufacture a threat just to create an enemy, giving those in power an opportunity to look like heroes for solving a problem that never existed to begin with. "Politicians are very aware of the fact that the heightened sense of control comes from both the enemy figure and the anxiety," he says.

This kind of fear changes our lives. In the 1980s, sociologists introduced the term "social capital" to describe the features of a community that enhance cooperation toward the mutual benefit of everyone in that community[10]—reciprocity, civic engagement, and other social norms. As one group put it, social capital "relates to the basic raw material of society." In 2006, sociologist Shannon Elizabeth Bell, then at the University of Oregon, sought to investigate the circumstances that diminish social capital. In particular she was interested in the influence that the coal industry had on communities in West Virginia, the second-highest coal producer in the US. She conducted interviews with forty people evenly split across two towns—one, a coal mining town, and the other, oriented around the poultry industry—asking them about trust within their community, the extent to which people helped each other out, and other similar questions. According to Bell's 2009 analysis, later published in her book *Fighting King Coal: The Challenges to Micromobilization in Central Appalachia*, residents of the coal mining town had a diminished sense of community compared to the other town. They distrusted each other, behaved less neighborly, and generally suffered a sense of disillusionment about their town. Interestingly, the town with less social capital had far more chain-link fences surrounding front yards—often locked. People there were more often afraid to leave their homes, and they kept their doors bolted.

Bell emphasizes that the breakdown of the community came before the fences and warning signs. But these physical markers—No Trespassing; Keep Out—reinforced that breakdown. They were, says Bell, now at Virginia Tech, "a visual cue of the low levels of social trust." As I read her study,

I was reminded of Milpa Verde in Brownsville, Texas, the neighborhood that abuts the border wall, where padlocked chain-link fences make ringing the doorbell to ask for help an impossibility.

And once we separate from one another, or decide that a community on the other side of a fence is an enemy, that mindset is hard to undo. As Sullivan points out, after apartheid was repealed in South Africa, many people continued to segregate themselves. "Sometimes the presence of a physical wall doesn't even matter," says Sullivan. "People will create it themselves."

All of this behavior is counter to what social research has found works best for coping with threats such as environmental or economic disasters. "Communities cope best when there are existing infrastructures of trust and cooperation," says Sullivan, "and people feel that they are looking out for each other." Such places tend to be much better prepared for emergency situations than those with stark divisions.

Living in fear is no way to live. But the consequences of this state of mind extend beyond coloring our daily experience of the place we live. For people experiencing the fear associated with border walls—whether owing to an immediate threat, like armed guards, or the subtler din of surveillance, or the even quieter but omnipresent fact of the system of control that walls are connected to—the eventual ramifications can be severe.

Stress, including that caused by fear due to approaching danger, can be good. It's a reaction that causes an immediate physical change: Our heart rate increases, and levels of stress hormones such as adrenaline and cortisol rise. These shifts help mobilize our body's resources so that we can respond; for example, breaking down fat so that we have more energy to escape the situation, and laying down memories so that we don't fall prey to the same danger in the future. Temporary stress also helps us learn to manage our lives. Children, for example, become better able to cope with, say, a shot at the pediatrician or frustration at not being able to do something, especially when the stressful experience happens against a background of support from parents or other caregivers. "The result is the development of healthy stress response systems," notes a 2005 paper by the National Scientific Council on the Developing Child, led by the Center on the Developing Child at Harvard University.

But decades of research, mostly in children, whose brains are still developing, have uncovered a definitive link between stress and health issues. The problem arises when the stress is prolonged. That is when positive stress turns to toxic stress. And toxic stress can harm the brain.

With short-lived stress, the amygdala, an almond-shaped collection of neurons contained deep in the brain, activates the body's response. The prefrontal cortex, in the brain's frontal lobe, regulates the amygdala by helping us appraise the situation and thereby modulate our emotions. Heightened activity in the prefrontal cortex leads to decreased activity in the amygdala; the better able we are to assess a situation, the faster we regulate our body's stress response.[11]

Prolonged stress can damage that tight-knit system, altering the architecture of the brain. Neural connections increase in regions responsible for fear, anxiety, and impulsive responses and decrease in regions related to reason, planning, and control. "You shift into a more reactive organism and a less reflective organism," says Megan Gunnar, who directs the Institute of Child Development at the University of Minnesota.

Weight gain is one consequence of this prolonged state. That makes sense, says Gunnar. Our biology is preparing to deal with a long-term emergency situation. "Your body has decided the world is harsh and unpredictable, so let's lay down fat stores because you never know when food will go away," she explains. The immune system goes on constant, low-grade alert. "It acts as if you're slightly wounded all the time," she says, probably so that it's ready to respond, seeing as our brains are delivering the message that danger is imminent. More broadly, toxic stress ages us, says Gunnar. She hypothesizes that this is a survival mechanism for the species: Considering we may not survive, we'd better get old enough to reproduce fast.[12]

Particularly among children, toxic stress can also lead to developmental issues. The hippocampus, a brain region vital to learning and memory, may be damaged when cortisol levels remain high for extended amounts of time. In the absence of a solid support system, cognitive performance may decline, notes Craig McEwen, a retired professor of economics and sociology at Bowdoin College, who began studying toxic stress late in his career with his brother, Bruce McEwen, a leading researcher in the field. Other studies have found links between this duet of dysregulation—a diminished prefrontal cortex and an exacerbated amygdala—and depression, anxiety disorders, aggression, and substance abuse.

The link between stress and childhood development has been well established in the context of poverty. According to a long-term study of forty-nine adults published in 2013, those with a lower family income at age nine had reduced activity in the prefrontal cortex and had trouble modulating their emotions by the time they were twenty-four.[13] "Early experiences of poverty," the researchers write, "become embedded within the organism, setting individuals on lifelong trajectories that portend morbidity."

Family turmoil, violence, perilous living conditions—these are the stressors that often accompany poverty. Although research has not examined the unique stress of living near a border wall, it's easy to make the leap. Fear, says Gunnar, triggers the same neurological cascade. Likewise, the lack of control also takes a toll. "Living in circumstances of uncertainty, which create anxiety and an inability to anticipate what might happen," says McEwen, "leads to toxic stress."

Not everyone who experiences prolonged stress responses develops the mental and physical issues research has identified. Some people thrive in stressful environments. Genetics plays a role. Above all, a supportive network formed by parents or other caregivers makes a huge difference. But again, the border wall shifts the balance. Children feel when parents are themselves living in fear. It's just a few steps removed from a parent physically disappearing. "There's nothing more terrifying to a kid," says Gunnar, than the prospect of a parent going missing. The images in the media of small

children separated from their parents at the US-Mexico border became a national nightmare for a reason. But parents
who haven't been taken away physically can still be taken
away emotionally when their environment is beyond their
control. "I think that would apply very well," says McEwen,
"to people living in the shadow of the wall."

5

Your Life Is Being Stopped Here
The Risk of Depression at the Border

BORDER WALLS ARE SAD PLACES. On the Mexican side of Friendship Park, paintings hung above the fence bring some color to the otherwise depressing architecture. *La poesía es gente con sueños*, reads one of them. "Poetry is people with dreams." Street musicians liven up the scene, too. But the ocean is just yards away and the sound of its waves is a constant reminder of a freedom unavailable to its human witnesses.

An estimated 7.5 million people live in the twenty-four US counties bordering Mexico. High rates of poverty and unemployment pervade these regions. People tend to be less educated and medical care is sparser.[1] One reassuring 2017 study in the *Journal of Immigrant and Minority Health* found that people living in the southern US borderlands were not more likely to report depression compared with people living elsewhere.[2] But another study from that same year found that almost a quarter of the 248 adult undocumented immigrants interviewed by psychologists at Rice University met the criteria for a mental disorder, a much higher rate than the general US population. Major depressive disorder was the most common diagnosis, but rates of panic and anxiety were also high.[3] And a report from Imperial County, California,

120 miles east of San Diego, noted that the area was rife with severe risk factors for poor mental health among youth: separation from parents, gang and other violence, fear that they or their parents will be deported, no medical insurance. Children who are recent immigrants face the additional obstacles of learning a new language, adjusting to a new school and new friends, and being teased.

A close look at the borderland counties of Texas reveals a disturbing pattern. About 18 percent of children throughout the state live in high-poverty neighborhoods. According to a 2017 report by the Center for Public Policy Priorities, now known as Every Texan, an independent public policy organization in Texas, that rate climbs to 68 percent in the Rio Grande Valley. Colonias, rural settlements along the border, home to an estimated 340,000 people,[4] often lack potable water, sewer systems, electricity, and paved roads. The median household income for Cameron and Hidalgo Counties, both along the border, is just over half of that for other counties in the state. An estimated 30 percent of children are undernourished. Adults in these counties, whether US-born or not, are less likely to hold high school diplomas than the adult population across the rest of the state.[5]

All of these factors contribute to the impact of living in a border region on children. A huge body of work demonstrates that adversity in childhood has long-lasting effects. The Adverse Childhood Experiences Study, or ACES, conducted by the Centers for Disease Control and Prevention, linked up to twenty-one million cases of depression with early-life experiences of violence, abuse, neglect, or family trauma.[6]

Poverty is, as we know, a major risk factor for mental health issues; this connection has been intimated for years. The landmark Whitehall Study, which tracked British civil servants over many years, found an undeniable link between social class and health: People with lower-status jobs had higher rates of heart disease and bronchitis.[7] And, as discussed in the previous chapter, researchers have zeroed in on the particularly damaging effects of poverty on children, whose brains are still forming. "Childhood socioeconomic status is associated with cognitive achievement throughout life," wrote psychologists Daniel Hackman and Martha Farah, of the Center for Cognitive Neuroscience at the University of Pennsylvania, in 2009. Studies have found that neurological systems governing language and executive function—mental skills that enable self-control, flexible thinking, planning, and focus—perform less adequately among children from poorer families compared with those from wealthier families. Although the research is sparse and scattered, imaging studies have also hinted at a link between socioeconomic status and brain function, and the data show that young children are hit the hardest by this connection.[8] Poverty also has physical consequences. Adult hypertension, arthritis, and activity limitations have all been linked to early-life poverty.[9]

Obviously, neighborhoods near border walls aren't the only places where these connections are borne out. But such problems are prevalent near border structures around the world. In 2016, researchers at Queen's University Belfast reported their analysis of health record data on 1.3 million people to see whether living near a peace line in Northern Ireland affected their mental health. They found that people living near segregation barriers were 19 percent more likely to hold a prescription for antidepressant medication compared with those living farther away from these separators. Prescriptions for anti-anxiety medication were 39 percent more common among people living near a barrier compared with those living farther away. Interestingly, the researchers, led by epidemiologist Aideen Maguire, found that when deprivation—in other words, poverty—was taken out of the mix, the difference subsided. Segregation was likely to lead to lower socioeconomic status, which in turn was likely to lead to mental health issues.

Social deprivation—the erosion of a healthy, vibrant relationship between people and society—is especially pronounced in peace wall areas. Signs of social deprivation in a community include higher rates of mental illness, alcohol use, a lack of upward economic mobility, and lower levels of education, among other factors. As one group wrote in 2014, "The most socially deprived areas in Belfast are also areas where 'peace walls' or interfaces between communities are prominent, are the areas of lowest educational attainment with the fewest amount of children and young people progressing into third level education, and are places where youth and unemployment run highest."[10] Fourteen of the twenty most deprived areas of Northern Ireland are near segregation barriers in an urban setting. Young people living near barriers have expressed reluctance to leave their community due to a fear of life "beyond the wall."

Clearly the situation in Northern Ireland involves more factors than merely whether or not people live near segregation barriers. But these structures connect to a painful history. "It is those individuals living in close proximity to a peace wall who are more likely to have had direct experience of violence than their counterparts living elsewhere in Northern Ireland," note the authors of a 2017 policy brief on the peace lines. More recent violence has tended to cluster around the barriers: 70 percent of all politically motivated murders in Belfast between 1996 and 2001 were committed within a third of a mile of a peace line. Rates of educational underachievement, unemployment, violence, alcohol abuse, and prescriptions for psychiatric medications—all are higher near the peace lines.

The physical barriers can't be held responsible as the sole cause of this clustered suffering. Many of the people experiencing these issues were born after the walls were built, so they have never known anything different. "The wall is simply part of the built environment," says Jonny Byrne, from Ulster University, an author of the previously mentioned and other related policy briefs.

And yet the cloud of problems hovering around the barriers is undeniable. "There's no doubt that the walls have created concentrated levels of social and economic and political deprivation," says Byrne. As with so many borders around the world, it's not just the physical structure that causes problems, but what the structure represents.

One of the strange truths about the peace lines, says Byrne, is that they worked. They accomplished the task they were built for, slowing down, even halting violence between communities. The peace lines even served as a model for concrete walls erected to stop attacks between the Sunnis and Shiites in Baghdad, Iraq, in the mid-2000s.[11] But the problem goes back to the fundamental problem with border walls: They create "the other." A barrier leads those behind it to adopt a single identity. And that identity is reinforced by stories and attitudes that treat those on the other side as dangerous, different, and inferior. "It becomes folklore," says Byrne, leading to stereotypes that pass from one generation to the next. By this time, the politicians who benefited from erecting the barriers are long gone; they don't have to deal with the lasting consequences. "When you build a wall, you have no idea what the environment's going to be like in twenty years' time," says Byrne. "The long-term effects are devastating."

So even though the barriers may have had some immediate benefit, Byrne sees nothing good about them. "Segregation isn't positive," he says. "Segregation is terrible." In a 2015 survey conducted by Byrne and others, nearly half of the one thousand respondents said they never interacted with communities on the other side of the nearest peace wall. More than half felt the barriers cast Northern Ireland in a negative light on the world stage. Although half the respondents said they wanted the walls removed, only a third of that half said they'd like them to come down right away. The rest of that half was less committal, wanting their removal "sometime in the future." And a third of the survey respondents wanted the walls to stay as they were. (The remainder wanted to keep the walls and either make them look nicer or improve access to the other side, or they didn't know what they thought.) The vast majority acknowledged that keeping the barriers in place would negatively affect jobs, safety, health and well-being, and community relations—all social factors that have been linked to diminished mental health.[12] As Byrne sees it, the proliferation of border walls around the world "tells us more about the absence of ideas to solve these problems."

Then there are the problems posed by the wall itself. "We are moving organisms," says trauma psychologist Bessel van der Kolk. Border walls immobilize us. This restriction can be devastating to our mental health. Van der Kolk recalls a disturbing observation he made as a medical student studying the brains of rats. Holding his hands over them to stop their movement proved traumatizing after just a minute or two. "The rats were messed up for the rest of their lives," he says.

Van der Kolk theorizes that the physical immobility imposed by border walls imparts a sense of being trapped and oppressed. That kind of traumatic feeling often roots itself in brain regions that we can't always access with language. And so instead of simply expressing how we feel, we become depressed, anxious, or filled with rage. These emotional reactions are reinforced by the presence of danger the wall signals. "How can you not get mental or physical illness from that?" says van der Kolk.

Mohammad Marie, a psychologist at Al-Najah National University in Nablus, in the Palestinian territories, sees the ramifications of this immobility daily. "It triggers fear and helplessness," he told me. Palestinians are already coping with adversities such as low income, unemployment, and land loss. The barrier, said Marie, reinforces the sense of being trapped within one's circumstances. This situation is complicated and nearly impossible to discuss in a satisfactory way. But in looking strictly and narrowly at the psychological impact of border walls, Palestinians bear undeniable consequences of the restriction and imposition of the walls surrounding them. This problem is not lost on many Israelis. "Palestinians in the Gaza Strip are fenced in, in a huge, huge prison," says Eli Somer. "The majority of people, who want to live a normal life, are prevented from doing so."

In 2009, researchers with Doctors Without Borders reported that among 1,254 mental health patients in the Gaza Strip and the West Bank, 23 percent reported post-traumatic stress disorder, 17 percent reported anxiety disorder, and 15 percent reported depression,[13] all of which the authors attributed to their experience of life in this region (witnessing murder or physical abuse; receiving threats; property destruction). Yet another study of 720 Palestinian teenagers in the West Bank reported that a quarter had attempted suicide.[14] Families report high levels of uncontrollable fear, hopelessness, depression, episodes of shaking, and insomnia among adults, along with bedwetting and excessive crying among children.[15] Marie told me that people throw themselves off the security barrier, fed up with life. "Depression is an epidemic problem here in Palestine," he said.

To be sure, the amount of trauma either witnessed or directly experienced is particularly high among Palestinians. In one study, 80 percent of more than 3,400 students in tenth and eleventh grade attending school in the Ramallah district of the West Bank said they had seen shootings, and nearly a third had seen a stranger killed. Half of the boys in this study had been body searched (presumably, by an Israeli soldier; the study does not specify) at some point in their lives.[16] These exposures exist in parallel to the border wall.

But the giant barrier at the edge of their territory, which reaches twenty-eight feet high in some areas, reinforces the sense of hopelessness every day. "It's not just a concrete prop," said Marie. "It represents that your life is being stopped here." Border walls make movement impossible. "When you stop moving," says van der Kolk, "you're dead."

6

A Big, Beautiful Wall
Why Looks Matter

THE ORIGINAL DIAGNOSIS of wall disease saw the structure itself as the cause. It was a bold connection to make. Could a slab of concrete, even one topped in barbed wire, really lead to delusion, paranoia, even schizophrenia? Now, emerging research on the neuroscience of architecture and aesthetics points in exactly that direction. The effects may not necessarily be as acute as those suffered by Müller-Hegemann's patients in the days of the Berlin Wall, but they are no less real. The evidence supports the notion that the design of a wall, and the wall's physical presence, can contribute to the psychological toll of life at the border.

A few years ago, University of Toronto psychologist Oshin Vartanian wanted to see if imaging technology would reveal preferences for different types of buildings. The question followed a line of inquiry begun at least two thousand years earlier, when Vitruvius, the Roman architect who wrote the ten-volume *De architectura*, outlined what he considered to be the three pillars of a good building: It must be structurally sound; it must be functional, serving the needs of its occupants; and it must be aesthetically appealing.

The aesthetics component has been a source of great interest over the centuries and around the world. The ornate carvings on a European church, the gentle light that passes through a Japanese rice paper screen, a Buddhist monastery seemingly carved right out of the cliffs—we want beauty in the buildings we erect around us.

The aesthetics of a structure hit us through our senses, through our knowledge, and through our emotions and values, each of which has a seat, or seats, in the brain. But why we like certain types of shapes, designs, and arrangements has been unclear, a question that psychologists, sociologists, neuroscientists, biologists, architects, and artists have all been drawn to try to answer. What they've found has much to say about the psychological toll of border walls.

Vartanian had study participants look at images of different building and spaces while inside an *f*MRI scanner. Functional magnetic resonance imaging works by showing changes in oxygen levels in different regions of the brain. When a region is working harder, it uses more oxygen. More oxygen requires an increase in the flow of blood to that region. This fluctuation causes a magnetic field change, which *f*MRI captures.

One set of images Vartanian used contained rooms with softer curves and rooms with harder angles. Somewhat predictably, most participants reported that they preferred the curves. The *f*MRI images showed that this preference connected to the brain's emotional circuitry. The curves made them feel better, says Vartanian. But he saw an even more dramatic response when he showed people pictures of closed spaces and open spaces. Temporal lobe regions of the brain involved in visual and spatial exploration became activated.[1] Activation of the anterior cingulate cortex also indicated a fear response when participants viewed the images of the closed spaces. The results reminded him of studies by Danish architect Lars Brorson Fich showing that people are better able to handle stressful situations when they are in an open space compared with when they are in a closed space.[2]

Tall buildings appear to have a similar effect on us. Robin Mazumder, a doctoral candidate in cognitive neuroscience at the University of Waterloo, has been trying to parse how urban design influences us psychologically. In one experiment, he asked people to rate the openness of various environments. Predictably, they rated environments populated by high-rise buildings as less open. But he took the inquiry further, asking them to assess how they were feeling by using a self-assessment manikin. This set of images aims to measure emotional response in terms of pleasure (does something have a positive or negative effect on our mood?), arousal (does it calm us or excite us?), and dominance (does it make us feel more or less in control?). By indicating which image matches their mood, study participants allow researchers a window into their psyche. The results, which are not yet published, were striking. Again and again, participants noted a change in the images corresponding with dominance. "When people look at environments with tall buildings," says Mazumder, "they have a lower sense of control."

Our preference for open spaces may be a matter of survival. In 1975, British geographer Jay Appleton introduced a theory he called prospect-refuge to explain why we like what we like in a landscape.[3] The theory builds on survival of the fittest, the notion introduced by Charles Darwin that life is driven by the need to survive, and those traits that make us fittest for our surroundings are the ones that will win that competition. Survival motivates us to seek habitats that offer both opportunity (prospect) and safety (refuge). For premodern humans, places like caves and savannas may have satisfied these requirements and thus enabled people to survive.

Appleton argues that this instinct now dictates what we find pleasing. Places where we can see what's around us, for example. Or places that minimize certain hazards. So we like vistas with wide views, hedges that we can hide behind and spy out from, peepholes that give us "the ability to see without being seen," as Appleton wrote. Architects have interpreted Appleton's theory to explain what pleases us in a building design. Open interiors offer prospect; enclosures offer refuge.

No published research has applied prospect-refuge theory to border walls, but it's not hard to make the leap. Walls cut off our view, thus impairing our sense of prospect, and their tall, flat surface offers no place for refuge. "People are less likely to want to be near environments that block their visibility," says Vartanian. "Being in an environment that you can't scan visually is threatening." Border walls leave people vulnerable to attack, as has happened to hundreds of people crossing between India and Bangladesh, and Georgians wandering too close to South Ossetia. They can leave us feeling locked, as people in the Palestinian territories have reported. They can lead to erroneous assessments of our surroundings, as seems to be the case with many people in Northern Ireland.

Viewed in terms of Vitruvius's three pillars of architecture, walls fulfill the requirement of being structurally sound. But their function does not serve the needs of people on both sides, and they aren't pretty. As earlier chapters have addressed, border walls are often part of a power dynamic foisted upon those they're designed to control. People may get used to the sight of them, even stop noticing them, or cover them with graffiti in protest or in an effort to beautify them. But that doesn't mean they aren't having an effect on people.

Thirty years ago, Joan Campbell, a public health specialist from Canada, introduced a concept called ambient stressors.[4] The term describes background noise and other interferences that we may not be aware of consciously but that take a toll on our well-being nonetheless. The hum of an air conditioner; pollution in the soil under our homes; fear of an explosion while living near a nuclear power plant—researchers have cited these as examples of ambient stressors. People live with these, often because, as one researcher wrote, "they consider the costs of coping with such stressors to be higher than simply enduring them."[5]

For many people, says Mazumder, border walls may be ambient stressors. And although people living nearby these structures may not notice them consciously, the stress they cause may eventually manifest in the same way as more acute types of stress. These problems are well known. Stress can lead to all manner of mental health issues, from depression to schizophrenia. The chronic stress of a border wall looming in the background could eventually push a person beyond what they can tolerate. The fact that this isn't an in-your-face type of stress could make it even more damaging, says Mazumder, "because you're not even aware that you're having this experience." It's a pattern that sounds an awful lot like the Mauerkrankheit of the Berlin Wall era.

The look of a border wall may also add to the stress. Joseph Fourier, a French mathematician who proposed the existence of the greenhouse effect back in the early 1800s, pioneered understandings about waves and frequencies that have been applied to many natural phenomena, including striped patterns on animals. Using his calculations, scientists have discerned that some stripes enable an animal to camouflage with their background; tigers are one example. As a result, their prey sees a singular image: tiger plus background combined. The two blend together. That never happens with human-made architecture. The pattern of windows and bricks in a skyscraper, for example, or the balconies jutting out of a tall apartment building, or the steps of an escalator—patterns like this are never present in a natural landscape. Psychologist Arnold Wilkins, emeritus professor at the University of Essex, found that patterns that depart from this rule of nature "take more effort for the brain to process."[6] Using a computer model, he and others found that the extent to which a building departs from a pattern that could occur in nature determines how uncomfortable people become when looking at it. "The brain needs more oxygen when uncomfortable scenes are observed," Wilkins told me. This may explain why people develop headaches when they look at tall buildings:

Headaches tend to be associated with excess oxygen usage. Extrapolating this phenomenon to border walls, we can see that their tall, repetitive designs may add yet another layer of stress to the people who live near them. Long stretches of concrete slabs, steel bollards, and coiled wire aren't organic. Thus, border walls, says Wilkins, "are more uncomfortable than natural images and rural scenes."

Other researchers have found that tall buildings can trigger an emotional state called behavioral freezing.[7] Such imposing structures may cause feelings of awe, note the Dutch researchers who uncovered this phenomenon. But that awe eventually gives way to feelings of smallness and oppression. This freezing, they write, "might discourage unwanted behavior in individuals." In other words, it can help control them.

Research is continuing to uncover the extent to which architecture influences our psychology, work that could prove extremely relevant to understanding the psychological toll of border walls. Zakaria Djebbara, who researches architecture and cognitive neuroscience at Aalborg University in Denmark, used virtual reality to see how people respond to various types of spaces. He found that people hesitated when they had to move through a narrow doorway to reach a goal, whereas they had no such trouble passing through a wide doorway. "The brain and body [do] not merely ask 'what do I perceive,' they also ask 'how can I act?'" Djebbara and colleagues write.[8] Border walls, says Djebbara, interrupt that process. "You're robbing people from moving from one place to another," he says. Put another way: Border walls steal futures.

Epilogue
The Border Within Us

"Borders are often pools of emotions, fears and memories," wrote the Finnish geographer Anssi Paasi in 2011.[1] Thirty years after the fall of the Berlin Wall, people who lived in its shadow still carry the scars. The *Mauer*, or wall, of wall disease, Mauerkrankheit, became unattached from the wall itself; now it's *die Mauer in den Köpfen*, the wall in the head. The concrete barrier that once separated and oppressed became an emotional barrier both between people and internally. The wall also became an easy metaphor to characterize and categorize people, continuing to define "the other" long after there was no other to define. The physical structure may have disappeared, but it had lived on far beyond its destruction because it now owned a corner of people's minds. This lasting impact is a cautionary tale if ever there was one. Considering the continued proliferation of border walls, there is no shortage of urgent need for its lessons.

Élisabeth Vallet, the geographer who has called attention to the proliferation of border walls around the world, notes how dramatically these structures alter the landscape. "The minute you build a wall, the functioning of that ecosystem changes," she says. The world a person knew is transformed, and usually without accomplishing anything constructive. "They don't solve the problems for which they have been built," she says, "and they trigger new problems." All they accomplish is to leave those who have to cope with them irrevocably changed.

On February 26, 2020, Ned Norris Jr., chairman of the Tohono O'odham Nation, a federally recognized tribe of up to thirty-four thousand members, testified before the House Committee on Natural Resources. The main reservation of the Tohono O'odham now borders Mexico for sixty-two miles. Two thousand members of the tribe live in Mexico. The historic homelands of the Tohono O'odham were split between the two countries when the border was drawn in 1854 (through a US purchase made a few years after the Mexican–American War ended) and extend far beyond the reservation, including Organ Pipe Cactus National Monument, the Cabeza Prieta National Wildlife Refuge, and other protected places. The bones of their ancestors are buried in areas targeted for the border wall.

At the very same time as Chairman Norris was offering testimony about the destruction of the sacred lands of his nation, the US Army detonated explosives at Organ Pipe Cactus National Monument, located in southern Arizona. The land had to be blasted in order to make way for wall construction. Eighty-six holes had been dug in the area, each ten feet deep, each containing five pounds of an explosive made of ammonium nitrate. "You'll hear a little bit of a thump," Jim Hug, an explosives expert with the Army Corps of Engineers, told a group of journalists that day. "Not a whole lot that's going to go on."[2]

Hundreds of miles away, in Washington, DC, the committee members and those providing testimony watched a video of another pre-wall blasting at a site sacred to the Tohono O'odham. Later, Norris responded to a question about why the sites being destroyed for the border wall were so important to his nation even though they were not on the reservation. "It's hard to see the blasting that you showed on the video today," Norris said, pausing to hold back tears, "because I know in my heart and what our elders have told us . . . that that area is home to our ancestors." Again he paused. "Blasting and doing what we saw today has totally disturbed, totally forever damaged our people."[3]

We internalize the fact of borders and the individual borders we live near. They influence our view of the world and our view of one another. The erection of a border wall irrevocably changes the lives of the people living up against them. Former habits like going to get ice cream or a haircut in the next town over come to an abrupt halt. Too often, what follows is the growth of suspicion, fear, depression, loss, and despair. None of this makes the world safer. And as the lesson of the Berlin Wall shows so clearly, even taking a border wall down doesn't guarantee a relief from these consequences. Vallet knows all too well the way a border becomes an unshakable, haunting presence. Once a wall goes up, she says, "The border is within you."

Notes

Introduction: Concrete, Steel, and Razor Wire

1 C. Leuenberger. "Constructions of the Berlin Wall: How Material Culture Is Used in Psychological Theory," *Social Problems* 53, no. 1, 18–37 (2006).

2 For a discussion in English of Müller-Hegemann's work on wall disease, see D. W. Winnicott, *Home Is Where We Start From: Essays by a Psychoanalyst* (New York: W. W. Norton, 1990).

3 "Celebration at the Berlin Wall," World News: Peter Jennings Reports Live from Berlin, November 10, 1989, youtube.com/watch?v=snsdDb7KDkg.

4 AFP, "Spirit of Optimism Is Gone: Sombre Mood as Germany Marks 30 Years of Berlin Wall Fall," *The Local Germany*, April 11, 2019.

5 Secure Fence Act of 2006, 109th Congress, Public Law 367. See also Fact sheet: The Secure Fence Act of 2006, georgewbush-whitehouse.archives.gov/news/releases/2006/10/20061026-1.html.

6 E. Vallet, "Border Walls and the Illusion of Deterrence," in *Open Borders: In Defense of Free Movement*, ed. R. Jones (Athens: University of Georgia Press, 2019).

7 S. Ramachandran, "The India-Bangladesh Wall: Lessons for Trump," *The Diplomat*, February 15, 2017.

8 R. Glennon, "The Unfolding Tragedy of Climate Change in Bangladesh," *Scientific American*, April 21, 2017.

9 "Coronavirus: Travel Restrictions, Border Shutdowns by Country," *Al Jazeera*, June 3, 2020.

10 Per travel restrictions by country, as listed at kayak.com/travel-restrictions.

1 | Sliding Down the Levee on Cardboard

1   R. Westerfelhaus, "She Speaks to Us, for Us, and of Us: Our Lady of Guadalupe as a Semiotic Site of Struggle and Identity," in *Communicating Ethnic and Cultural Identity*, eds. M. Fong and R. Chuang (Lanham, Md.: Rowman & Littlefield, 2004).

2   M. Lester, *Sacred Journeys: Your Guide to the World's Most Transformative Spaces, Places and Sites* (New York: Adams Media, 2019).

3   J. Porterfield, *The Treaty of Guadalupe Hidalgo, 1848: A Primary Source Examination of the Treaty That Ended the Mexican–American War* (New York: Rosen, 2006).

4   J. Duda, *If This Be Treason: The American Rogues and Rebels Who Walked the Line Between Dissent and Betrayal* (Guilford, Conn.: Globe Pequot/Lyons Press, 2017).

5   *Routledge Handbook of Chicana/o Studies*, eds. F. A. Lomelí, D. A. Segura, E. Benjamin-Labarthe (London: Routledge,2018).

6   Virginia Randolph Trist to Tockerman, July 8, 1864, Nicholas P. Trist Papers, Box 10, Library of the University of North Carolina at Chapel Hill. See also Robert W. Drexter, *Guilty of Making Peace: A Biography of Nicholas P. Trist* (Lanham, Md.: University Press of America, 1991), 139.

7   Duda, *If This Be Treason*, op. cit.

8   See also friendshippark.org for a complete history of this border-straddling park.

9   US Customs and Border Protection, Border Patrol History, cbp.gov/border-security/along-us-borders/history.

10   K. Davis, "Operation Gatekeeper at 25: Look Back at the Turning Point That Transformed the Border," *Los Angeles Times*, September 30, 2019.

11   American Immigration Council, Fact Sheet: The Cost of Immigration Enforcement at the Border, July 2020.

12   T. Sanchez, "Deported Mothers Make New Lives in Tijuana," *San Diego Union-Tribune*, August 21, 2016.

13   B. L. Brush, L. E. Gultekin, E. B. Dowdell, et al., "Understanding trauma normativeness, normalization, and help seeking in homeless mothers," *Violence Against Women* 24, no. 13: 1523–39 (2018).

14   N. Miroff, A. Blanco, "Trump Ramps Up Border-Wall Construction Ahead of 2020 Vote," *The Washington Post*, February 6, 2020.

15 National Butterfly Center, "National Butterfly Center Obtains Temporary Restraining Order against Brian Kolfage and We Build the Wall," December 4, 2019, nationalbutterflycenter.org/nbc-multi-media/in-the-news/286-national-butterfly-center-obtains-temporary-restraining-order-against-brian-kolfage-and-we-build-the-wall.

16 L. Guerra, "I Voted for Trump. Now His Wall May Destroy My Butterfly Paradise," *The Washington Post*, December 17, 2018.

17 S. Inskeep, "Will President Trump's Border Wall Keep Drugs Out of the U.S.?" National Public Radio, February 20, 2019.

18 A. Gomez, "Fact-Checking Trump Officials: Most Drugs Enter US through Legal Ports of Entry, Not Vast, Open Border," *USA Today*, January 16, 2019.

2 | The Wall in the Brain

1 S. Ostrovsky, "The Russians Are Coming: Georgia's Creeping Occupation," VICE News, November 14, 2015.

2 S. Ostrovsky, "A Decade After Russia War, Plight of Georgian Refugees Continues," *Arab News/AFP*, August 5, 2018.

3 M. Mulcey (L. Perrier, trans.), "A World Tour of States Not Recognized by the UN," *Le Journal International*, July 9, 2015.

4 M. Chechlacz, G. W. Humphreys, "The Enigma of Bálint's Syndrome: Neural Substrates and Cognitive Deficits," *Frontiers in Human Neuroscience* 8, article 123 (2014).

5 J. M. S. Pearce, "Sir Gordon Holmes (1876–1965)," *Journal of Neurology, Neurosurgery & Psychiatry* 75, no. 10: 1502–3 (2004).

6 G. Holmes, "The Montgomery Lectures in Ophthalmology, Lecture 1: The Cortical Localization of Vision," *British Medical Journal*, August 16, 1919: 193–99.

7 S. Corkin, *Permanent Present Tense: The Unforgettable Life of the Amnesic Patient, H. M* (New York: Basic Books, 2013).

8 J. O'Keefe, "Spatial Cells in the Hippocampal Formation," Nobel Lecture, December 7, 2014.

9 Ibid.

10 Ibid.

11   E. Moser, M.-B. Moser, B. McNaughton, "Spatial Representation in the Hippocampal Formation: A History," *Nature Neuroscience* 20, 1448–64 (2017).

12   C. Leuenberger, "From the Berlin Wall to the West Bank Barrier: How Material Objects and Psychological Theories Can Be Used to Construct Individual Cultures and Traits," in *After the Berlin Wall: Germany and Beyond*, eds. K. Gerstenberger and J. E. Braziel (New York: Palgrave Macmillan, 2011).

13   Ostrovsky, *Arab News/AFP*, op. cit.

14   A. North, "Russian Expansion: 'I Went to Bed in Georgia—and Woke Up in South Ossetia,'" *The Guardian*, May 20, 2015.

15   "The Man Trapped in Frozen Limbo," CNN, Jan 6, 2017, cnn.com/videos/world/2017/01/06/russia-georgia-border-limbo-victim-sdg-orig.cnn.

16   O. Bratfisch, "Further Study of the Relational Between Subjective Distance and Emotional Involvement," *Acta Psychologica* 29, 244–55 (1969).

17   C.-C. Carbon, H. Leder, "The Wall Inside the Brain: Overestimation of Distances Crossing the Former Iron Curtain," *Psychonomic Bulletin & Review* 12, 746–50 (2005).

18   D. Xiao, Y. Liu, "Study of Cultural Impacts on Location Judgments in Eastern China," *Lecture Notes in Artificial Science* 4736, 20–31 (2007).

19   B. P. Meier, A. C. Moller, J. J. Chen, M. Riemer-Peltz, "Spatial Metaphor and Real Estate: North-South Location Biases Housing Preference," *Social Psychological and Personality Science* 2, no. 5: 547–53 (2011).

20   L. D. Nelson, J. P. Simmons, "On Southbound and Northbound Fees: Literal Consequences of the Metaphoric Link between Vertical Position and Cardinal Direction," *Journal of Marketing Research* 46, no. 6: 715–24 (2009).

3 | The Other Side of the Border

1   "Forensic Architecture Investigation: Herbicidal Warfare in Gaza," forensic-architecture.org/investigation/herbicidal-warfare-in-gaza.

2   K. Dickson, "The Wall of Uruk: Iconicities in Gilgamesh," *Journal of Ancient Near Eastern Religions* 9, no. 1: 25–50 (2009).

3   K. D'Costa, "The (Anthropological) Truth about Walls," *Scientific American*, February 7, 2017.

4   B. P. Alcaide, "The Great Wall of China's Long Legacy," *National Geographic*, December 2018.

5   Aelianus Spartianus, Life of Hadrian, in *Historia Augusta*, c. 300 CE.

6   J. Agnew, "Borders on the Mind: Reframing Border Thinking," *Ethics & Global Politics* 1, no. 4: 175–91 (2008).

7   J. Gulddal, C. Payne, "Passports: On the Politics and Cultural Impact of Modern Movement Control," *symploke* (Lincoln: University of Nebraska Press) 25, nos. 1–2: 9–23 (2017).

8   A. Levine, "Before the Great War, People Travelled Freely without Passports or Identification," *Winnipeg Free Press*, August 18, 2014.

9   M. Walker, J. Sindreu, "Passports: 100 Years Legacies: The Lasting Impact of World War I," *Wall Street Journal*, June 28, 2014.

10 G. Pines, "The Contentious History of the Passport," *National Geographic*, May 16, 2017.

11 D. Turack, "Freedom of Movement and the International Regime of Passports," *Osgoode Hall Law Journal* 6, no. 2: 230–51 (1968).

12 Article 23, The Covenant of the League of Nations (Art. 1 to 26), The Paris Peace Conference 1919, history.state.gov/historicaldocuments/frus1919Parisv13/ch10subch1.

13 Passport Conference Preparatory Documents, League of Nations, Advisory and Technical Committee for Communications and Transit, Geneva, November 1, 1925.

14 Turack, *Osgoode Hall Law Journal*, op. cit.

15 Ibid.

16 Ibid.

17 The Universal Declaration of Human Rights, United Nations, December 10, 1948.

18 This conflict has been reported widely and several news outlets have also published explanatory background articles. For example, see S. Saifa, S. Gupta, I. Mir, J. Hollingsworth, "The Terrified Kashmir Families Who Call One of the World's Most Militarized Zones Home," CNN, October 27, 2019; and "Kashmir: Why India and Pakistan Fight," BBC, August 8, 2019.

19 S. Snow, "Analysis: Why Kashmir Matters," *The Diplomat*, September 19, 2016.

20 D. A. Mahapatra, "From Alienation to Co-existence and Beyond: Examining the Evolution of the Borderland in Kashmir," *Journal of Borderland Studies* 33, no. 1: 141–55 (2016).

21 Mahapatra, *Journal of Borderland Studies*, op. cit.

22 This assertion is based on interviews and media coverage of the situation among Georgia, South Ossetia, and Russia.

23 This statement is based on the extensive reporting on the situation in this region.

24 P. Collison, *The Cuttleslowe Walls: A Study in Social Class* (London: Faber and Faber, 1963).

25 W. H. McNeill, "Frederick the Great and the Propagation of Potatoes," in *I Wish I'd Been There—Book Two: European History*, eds. B. Hollinshead and T. K. Rabb (New York: Anchor Books, 2009).

26 M. Janetsky, "Lima's 'Wall of Shame' and the Art of Building Barriers," *The Atlantic*, September 7, 2019.

27 The economic disparity associated with the wall in Lima has been widely reported. For example, see "Peru's 'Wall of Shame' Keeping Rich and Poor Apart," Al Jazeera English, November 29, 2015, youtube. com/watch?v=v2fRdPWmfaw; and "Peru: Wall of Shame," ARTE Documentary, October 18, 2018, youtube.com/watch?v=WaORq10lOio.

28 For one example of this widely covered development, see A. Smale, "Migrants Race North as Hungary Builds a Border Fence," *The New York Times*, August 24, 2015.

29 R. Lyman, H. Bienvenu, "Migrants Clash with Police in Hungary, as Others Enter Croatia," *The New York Times*, September 16, 2015.

30 M. A. Kallius, "The Speaking Fence," *Anthropology Now* 9, no. 3: 16–23 (2017).

31 Belfast Interface Project, belfastinterfaceproject.org/interfaces-map.

32 D. Morrow, C. Gormley-Heenan, J. Byrne, M. Rosato, S. Cook, "Analysing Baseline Data on Peace Walls (6): Implications for Policy: Policy Brief," Ulster University Institute for Research in Social Sciences, November 2017.

4 | Mortal Danger

1 For one story on this widely covered incident, see R. Dasgupta, "With SC Set to Hear Petition, Killings at Bangladesh Border Back in Focus," *The Wire*, March 5, 2020.

2 "Indian Court Sets March 18 for Hearing after 5 Years," *New Age Bangladesh*, February 15, 2020. In early 2020, Felani Khatun's father

petitioned the Indian high court to ask for a third trial. That hearing was scheduled for March 18, 2020. As of the publication of this book, no further news was available about this petition.

3   For one report, see M. Sattar, "Bangladesh-India Border: 'Wall of Death,'" *The World*, Public Radio International, January 4, 2012.

4   B. Adams, "India's Shoot-to-Kill Policy on the Bangladesh Border," *The Guardian*, January 23, 2011.

5   "Fighting Boko Haram in Chad: Beyond Military Measures," International Crisis Group, Report No. 246, March 8, 2017.

6   S. Denyer, "Wildlife Thrives among the Land Mines along Korea's DMZ. But for How Long?" *The Washington Post*, August 27, 2019.

7   For one such incident, see C. Sang-Hun, "North Korean Soldier Shot by Own Troops as He Defects to the South," *The New York Times*, November 13, 2017.

8   A photograph of the sign can be seen online at electronicintifada.net/content/psychological-implications-israels-separation-wall-palestinians/1538.

9   P. Rucker, "'How Do You Stop These People?': Trump's Anti-Immigrant Rhetoric Looms over El Paso Massacre," *The Washington Post*, August 4, 2019.

10 S. E. Bell, "'There Ain't No Bond in Town Like There Used To Be': The Destruction of Social Capital in the West Virginia Coalfields," *Sociological Forum* 24, no. 3: 631–57 (2009).

11 P. Kim, G. W. Evans, M. Angstadt, et al., "Effects of Childhood Poverty and Chronic Stress on Emotion Regulatory Brain Function in Adulthood," *PNAS* 110, no. 46: 18442–47 (2013).

12 A selection of the many studies on the connections between poverty, stress, childhood development and adult health: Kim et al., *PNAS*, op. cit.; K. Koss, M. R. Gunnar, "Annual Research Review: Early Adversity, the Hypothalamic-Pituitary-Adrenocortical Axis, and Child Psychopathology," *Journal of Child Psychology & Psychiatry* 59, no. 4: 327–46 (2018); P. M. Miguel, L. O. Pereira, P. P. Silveira, M. J. Meaney, "Early Environmental Influences on the Development of Children's Brain Structure and Function," *Developmental Medicine & Child Neurology* 61, no. 10: 1127–33 (2019); "Excessive Stress Disrupts the Architecture of the Developing Brain: Working Paper 3," National Scientific Council on the Developing Child, 2005, updated 2014, developingchild.harvard.edu.

13 Kim et al., *PNAS*, op. cit.

5 | Your Life Is Being Stopped Here

1   P. A. C. Vaeth, R. Caetano, B. A. Mills, "Factors Associated with Depression among Mexican Americans Living in US-Mexico Border and Non-Border Areas," *Journal of Immigrant and Minority Health* 18, no. 4: 718–27 (2016).

2   Vaeth et al., *Journal of Immigrant and Minority Health*, op. cit.

3   L. M. Garcini, J. M. Peña, T. Galvan, et al., "Mental Disorders among Undocumented Mexican Immigrants in High-Risk Neighborhoods: Prevalence, Comorbidity, and Vulnerabilities," *Journal of Consulting and Clinical Psychology* 85, no. 10: 927–36 (2017).

4   R. Peterson, "Texas' Colonias: Squatter Settlements Become Affordable Housing," *Urban Ecology Journal*, urbanecology.org/texas-colonias-squatter-settlements-affordable-housing.

5   "State of Texas Children 2017: Child Well-Being in the Rio Grande," Center for Public Policy Priorities, Texas Kids Count Project, forabettertexas.org/images/2017_SOTC_RioGrande.pdf.

6   "Adverse Childhood Experiences: Fast Facts," National Center for Injury Prevention and Control, Division of Violence Prevention, Centers for Disease Control and Prevention, cdc.gov/violenceprevention/childabuseandneglect/aces/fastfact.html.

7   M. G. Marmot, S. Stansfeld, C. Patel, et al., "Health Inequalities among British Civil Servants: The Whitehall II Study," *The Lancet* 337, no. 8754: 1387–93 (1991).

8   D. A. Hackman, M. J. Farah, "Socioeconomic Status and the Developing Brain," *Trends in Cognitive Sciences* 13, no. 2: 65–73 (2009).

9   W. T. Boyce, M. B. Sokolowsky, G. E. Robinson, "Toward a New Biology of Social Adversity," *PNAS* 109, Supplement 2: 17143–48 (2012).

10 A. Maguire, D. French, D. O'Reilly, "Residential Segregation, Dividing Walls and Mental Health: A Population-Based Record Linkage Study," *Journal of Epidemiology and Community Health* 70, no. 9: 845–54 (2016).

11 J. Byrne, C. Gormley-Heenan, D. Morrow, M. Rosato, S. Cook, "Analysing Baseline Data on Peace Walls (5): Exploring the Socio-Economic, Education and Employment Factor: Policy Brief," Ulster University Institute for Research in Social Sciences, November 2017.

12   H. McDonald, "Belfast-Style Peace Walls Recommended for Baghdad,"
     The Guardian, September 14, 2007.

13   J. Byrne, C. Gormley-Heenan, D. Morrow, B. Sturgeon, "Public
     Attitudes to Peace Walls (2015): Survey Results," Ulster University,
     2015.

14   E. Espie, V. Gaboulaud, T. Baubet, et al., "Trauma-Related Psychological
     Disorders among Palestinian Children and Adults in Gaza and West
     Bank, 2005–2008," *International Journal of Mental Health Systems* 3,
     no. 1: 21–25 (2009).

15   F. Ghrayeb, M. Rusli, M. Ismail, A. Al Rifai, "Prevalence of Suicide
     Ideation and Attempt among Palestinian Adolescents: Across-
     Sectional Study," *World Journal of Medical Sciences* 10, no. 3: 261–66
     (2014).

16   R. Giacaman, A. Husseini, N. Gordon, F. Awartani, "Imprints on the
     Consciousness," *European Journal of Public Health* 14, no. 3: 286–90
     (2004).

17   R. Giacaman, H. S. Shannon, H. Saab, N. Arya, W. Boyce, "Individual
     and Collective Exposure to Political Violence: Palestinian Adolescents
     Coping with Conflict," *European Journal of Public Health* 17, no. 4:
     361–68 (2007).

6 | A Big, Beautiful Wall

1   A. Cobrun, O. Vartanian, A. Chatterjee, "Buildings, Beauty and the
     Brain: A Neuroscience of Architectural Experience," *Journal of
     Cognitive Neuroscience*, May 11, 2017: 1–11.

2   L. Brorson Fich, A. Hansen, A. H. Garde, L. Petrini, P. Jönsson, "Can the
     Design of Space Alter Stress Responses?" Conference of the Academy
     of Neuroscience for Architecture, September 23, 2016.

3   A. Dosen, M. Ostwald, "Prospect and Refuge Theory: Constructing a
     Critical Definition for Architecture and Design," *International Journal
     of Design in Society* 6, no 1: 9–23 (2013).

4   J. M. Campbell, "Ambient Stressors," *Environment & Behavior* 15, no 3:
     355–80 (1983).

5   G. W. Evans, "Crowding and Other Environmental Stressors," in
     International Encyclopedia of the Social & Behavioral Sciences, eds. N. J.
     Smelser and P. B. Baltes (Oxford, UK: Pergamon Press, 2001).

6 A. J. Wilkins, "Looking at Buildings Can Actually Give People Headaches—Here's How," *The Conversation*, June 1, 2017.

7 Y. Joye, S. Dewitte, "Up Speeds You Down. Awe-Evoking Monumental Buildings Trigger Behavioral and Perceived Freezing," *Journal of Environmental Psychology* 47, 112–25 (2016).

8 Z. Djebbara, L. B. Fich, K. Gramann, "Understanding Perceptual Experience of Art Using Mobile Brain/Body Imaging," in *Brain Art: Brain-Computer Interfaces for Artistic Expression*, ed. A. Nijholt (Basel: Springer Nature Switzerland AG, 2019).

Epilogue: The Border Within Us

1 A. Passi, "A Border Theory: An Unattainable Dream or a Realistic Aim for Border Scholars?" *The Ashgate Research Companion to Border Studies*, ed. D. Wastl-Walter (Farnham, Surrey, UK: Ashgate, 2011).

2 R. Devereaux, "The Border Patrol Invited the Press to Watch It Blow Up a National Monument," *The Intercept*, February 27, 2010.

3 "Subcommittee Hearing: Destroying Sacred Sites and Erasing Tribal Culture: The Trump Administration's Construction of the Border Wall," National Resources Committees, February 26, 2020.

Acknowledgments

Thank you to all of the people—academic researchers, psychologists, other professionals and several citizens of Brownsville and Mission, Texas—who spoke and corresponded with me for this book. Your generosity made this book possible. These individuals include: John Agnew, Ruth Alejos, Anthony Asiwaju, Rey Anzaldua, Shannon Bell, Sam Bishop, Jonny Byrne, Claus-Christian Carbon, Fred Cavazos, Zakaria Djebbara, Arlene Ducao, Ahmad El-Atrash, Ryan Enos, İlker Erkan, Talfan Evans, Reverend John Fanestil, Juliet Garcia, Gabrielle Girardeau, Tasha Golden, Luciano Guerra, Megan Gunnar, Trinidad Gonzalez, Dafna Hirsch, Gilad Hirschberger, Kate Jeffery, Reece Jones, Francisco Lara-Valencia, Christine Leuenberger, Aideen Maguire, Frederick Marks, Robin Mazumdar, Craig McEwen, Gela Merabishvili, Mohamad Meri, Samaneh Moafi, Edvard Moser, David Navarrete, Scott Nicol, Samuel Okunade, Hayden O'Shaughnessy, Nancy Pacheco, Tako Robakidze, Juan Rodriguez, Eli Somer, Daniel Sullivan, Abigail Thornton, Gerard Toal, Marianna Trevino-Wright, Élisabeth Vallet, Bessel van der Kolk, Oshin Vartanian, Tobias Vogt, Vamik Volkan and. Eyal Weizman, However, any errors or missteps in this book are mine alone and do not reflect on any of the people named here.

Thank you to my editor, Nick Cizek, for the initial vision for this book and everything that followed. Also at The Experiment, thank you to Matthew Lore and Zach Pace. Thank you to Anne Horowitz for masterful copyediting and to Ann Kirschner for careful proofreading. Thank you to Joshua Rothman, editor at *The New Yorker*, for saying yes to the original idea to explore the psychological toll of border walls.

Thank you to my family for being my family, and thank you especially to my love, Lloyd Sherman, for being so caring and encouraging.

Index

About the Author

JESSICA WAPNER is a journalist and former science editor at *Newsweek* whose work has appeared in *The New Yorker*, *The New York Times*, *Wired*, *Medium*, *Discover*, *Popular Science*, *Self*, *Scientific American*, *New York* magazine, *The Atlantic*, and elsewhere. Her first book, *The Philadelphia Chromosome*, was named a top ten nonfiction book by *The Wall Street Journal*. She lives in Brooklyn.

jessicawapner.com | @jessicawapner